AF227663

MEET THE PARENTS

MARYANN JONES THOMPSON
Founder & Editor in Chief

MARIA DE LA O
Executive Editor

DIDRIK JOHNCK
Photographer at Large

SARAH HART, DINA HARRISON, MEGAN HARVEY, EMILY JANOWSKY
Contributing Editors

SHELLEY FARGO, JESSICA EDELEN
Copy Editors

CRYSTAL ENGSTROM
Photo Editor

KARLA CLAYTON
Print Design

PATRICK YORE
Web Design

WENDY MCKINLEY
Web Production

CALIFORNIAN GUIDES
Publisher

Contributors
AMY ALLEN
VALENTINE J. BRKICH
LILIIA DECOS
HEATHER EDWARDS
STEPHANIE FRIAS
JODI GLASSER
DENNIS HARRISON
JENNIFER HARRISON
JILL HEADLEY
CAROLYN JENSEN
MARGARET JONES
AMY JORDAN JONES
CLAIRE KERR-ZLOBIN
ERIN KIRKLAND
MARLIEKE KROON
DARYA MEAD
HEATHER MUNDT
BELINDA O'NEIL
BETHANY PHILLIPS
NICOLA "POZ" POSWILLO
PAUL PUNTOUS
JULIE RAPPAPORT
RENEE SIEGEL
LEAH SOLTER
DON THOMPSON
ELIZABETH WEINGART
CULLEN WIGINTON

Cover Photo
CULLEN WIGINTON

Back Cover Photo
DON THOMPSON

ROAM was created by real parent travelers who explored a small corner of the world with their children and want to share their experience and know-how with other families.

ROAM
FIND YOUR ADVENTURE

TIPS & TRICKS FOR BETTER TRIPS
Advice from veteran parent travelers

ADVENTURE

Turning "Vacation" into "Adventure"
P _ 1 1

PLANNING

How to tackle Europe with kids **P _ 1 2**

GEAR

Editor's picks for Gear of the Year
P _ 1 3

PACKING

The secret to the perfectly packed family **P _ 1 4**

ON THE ROAD

Ways to keep both parents and kids happy **P _ 1 5**

PHOTOS

Winning travel photographers share their secrets **P _ 1 6**

TECH

Must-have apps for avid travelers
P _ 1 7

1 COLOMBIA

A Rebirth of Plazas, Playas & People

P _ 2 0

ROAM'S
19 FOR 2019
The most exciting vacations of the year

2 ARGENTINA

Glacial Perfection in Patagonia
P _ 2 4

3 OREGON

Adventuring by Airstream **P _ 2 7**

4 CAMBODIA

Way More than Angkor **P _ 3 0**

5 SPAIN

The Sublimity of San Sebastián
P _ 3 3

6 MICRONESIA

Manta-Hunting on the Reefs of Yap **P _ 3 6**

7 INDIA

Himalayan Trekking with the Women of Ladakh **P _ 3 9**

8 TANZANIA

The Toughest Kilimanjaro Climb
P _ 4 2

9 CROATIA

The Coast by Catamaran
P _ 4 5

10 IDAHO

Rafting Heaven in Hell's Canyon **P _ 4 8**

MORE AMAZING & UNFORGETTABLE ADVENTURES
A full year of family vacation time together

ROAM'S 2019
Best Family Travel Photos

ROAM
WITH US

Denali

From rafting to relaxing and from epic treks to weekend getaways, ROAM contributors have crisscrossed the globe and share their most exciting travel tales in the pages of this issue.

TIPS & TRICKS
FOR BETTER TRIPS
FROM THE PARENTS
WHO'VE BEEN THERE

HOW TO TURN A VACATION INTO AN ADVENTURE

ROAM covers out-of-the-box trips for families. What makes an extraordinary vacation? Here's the kind of traveling our editors love.

New A place both parents and kids are exploring for the first time, together.

Custom The best experiences are not plug-and-play; some amount of independent planning is required.

Valuable Whether cheap or expensive, all adventures deliver value for the money.

Active Just sitting on a tour bus or in the backseat doesn't qualify.

Scary Feeling a bit nervous about some aspect of the trip is a good sign.

If you're new to independent traveling but want to add a bit of spice to your next family trip, you can ease into the pool of adventure without being forced to jump in the deep end. Start with a visit to a friend living overseas, booking a family tour, or using a travel agent. They'll be able to match your appetite for adventure, safety, comfort and expense with a vacation you'll crave.

THE MOST MEMORABLE TRIPS ARE NOT PLUG-AND-PLAY

FINDING FIRSTS

"It's hard to describe the feeling of watching our seven-year-old top out after his first 75-foot climb. When this little dude got vertical, his focus, commitment, and problem-solving were on full display. Heavy rains had forced all the climbers under one overhang to find dry rock. He got stuck on a problem for quite a while near the top, but when he got past it, the two dozen folks watching from below erupted in hoots and hollers." – Didrik Johnck

Read more:
bit.ly/roam2019thailand

PLANNING

HOW TO TACKLE EUROPE

What you loved about Europe as a twenty-something backpacker won't be what works with your kids: Museums, shopping, bars, long meals, people watching — these activities are the bane of children's lives. After making our way across many of the most popular European destinations over the past three summers, we've come up with some strategies for crafting a fun family itinerary.

You choose the destination. Figure out what countries you want to visit and what appeals to you. Then work on drumming up interest with the kids. If you're happy, they'll be happy.

Involve the kids. Show your children photos, books, and maps about where you're going. After a few trips, my kids now read the *Lonely Planet* children's books about the countries we're aiming for. I ask them to pick one spot that interests them, and sometimes I have to say "sorry" when a cool spot is too far away.

Alternate city and country. We typically spend 4–5 days in a big city where there is a lot to see, then move to a beach or mountain town for relaxing and recharging. In ten days, we did Barcelona and Costa Brava for some beach time, which was a perfect mix.

Minimize travel days. During that Barcelona trip, we were tempted to add northern Spain but that would have burnt most of a day traveling. To Americans, everywhere in Europe seems so close that it is tempting to add more and more cities to the itinerary.

Consider how much time you'll spend traveling to the place vs. being in the place. Ideally, stay 3 nights in one place, minimum, and keep travel days to less than 10 percent of your trip.

Minimize "climate" changes. Beach + fancy city + mountains = too many clothes to pack. If you've got to slice something from your itinerary, consider sticking with two "climates."

Adjust to local schedules. In "night owl" places like France and Spain, we tend to sleep until late morning, return for a midafternoon siesta, and stay up well past midnight. If you can immediately match the schedule of the locals, you won't miss out on any of the fun (and what kid doesn't want to stay up past midnight?!)

Don't bite off too much. If you try to do everything there is to do in a city like, say, London, you'll burn out — and your kids will be so miserable watching you be so stressed that they won't develop a love of travel. Pick your top 3–5 things that you want to see in each city. Then see just those — and don't jam them all in one day, either!

Buy advance tix for big stuff. The main sights in Europe are mobbed with tourists all year long. As soon as you know which three days you'll be in Rome, book the Vatican Museum tour for that first day, and so on.

Do "boring" mornings. After grabbing a bite of breakfast, we try to do our most "adult" activity first. Whether it is a museum, church, or historical site, the kids will be most awake, least whiny and not yet have tired feet.

Tour by bike. If your kids get whiny after a lot of days of walking around a big city, book a bike tour for a change of pace.

No plans? No worries. I'll be honest. Though some of my friends book months in advance, we tend to book our summer travels at the last minute — up to two months in advance, max. (Keep in mind, however, that Europe in August can be impossibly full, and even June and July seaside spots tend to fill up by May.)

We watch for the best deals and stay flexible about where to start our trip. After all, it's Europe — you can't go wrong. It's all good! *— Dina Harrison*

IF YOU'RE HAPPY, THEY'LL BE HAPPY

YEAR OF THE BLACK HOLE

Photograph, schmotograph. My go-to black hole is much closer to home than 318 quintillion miles away. When I need a bag big enough for a family and tough enough to endure campgrounds, rainforests, safaris, and United's lost baggage storage facility, I get one of my **Patagonia Black Hole Bags.** When packing for a recent trip to Baja, I had so much gear set out, I didn't think there was any way it could all fit inside my 60-liter duffel. But, man, it did! Now, Patagonia has expanded the line to include the world's toughest toiletry bag, versions with backpack straps and wheels, as well as some made from lighter-weight material. The only bummer is that these bags are getting so popular, you might need to tie a goofy yarn ribbon to the handle to be sure you're grabbing yours off the luggage carousel. *— Paul Puntous*

Read more: bit.ly/roam2019gear

PACKING

THE SECRET TO THE PERFECTLY PACKED FAMILY

What's the secret to easy packing for family trips? Compartmentalize. Compartmentalize. Compartmentalize. And the secret to compartmentalization? Packing cubes.

Even though our kids are old enough to carry their own bags, we like to pack light. Having four large packs would just allow us to overpack (and give us more to carry when we have to run through the airport to make a connecting flight).

Packing cubes give each person their own clothes bag to manage. Our primary cubes are actually a shoe-boxy rectangle that unzips on three sides, which makes it both easy to pack and easy to see the entire contents.

I like the cubes made out of old-fashioned backpack material, which gives them a bit of structure even when empty — but there are countless varieties to choose from.

With each person's clothes packed in a cube, we organize the rest of our family's gear into other packing cubes — one or two for toiletries, one for jackets/hats, one for medicine, one for tech/camera gear, etc. In total, we leave home with about ten cubes to hold everything.

When we arrive at a hotel for the night, we only pull out the cubes we need. One night? Just clothes and toiletries. Several nights? Dump the whole pack. For families traveling on road trips or jumping through cities in Europe, packing cubes are time-and sanity-savers. — *Maryann Jones Thompson*

Carlos Frias

4 WAYS TO KEEP THE PEACE

Dragging me around an expensive amusement park leaves me as unhappy as my kids would be if we dragged them around for a day of wine tasting. ROAM contributors have found success incorporating these "peacemakers" into their itineraries to keep everyone as content as possible on the road.

1 **Water.** The promise of a splash in the water is something both kids and adults can get behind. Visiting Angkor Wat in blistering heat, we constantly reminded our kids of the pool awaiting them after the next temple. This is a great tip to keep in mind when visiting big cities: Don't forget to book a place with a pool.

2 **Rest days.** We've found our kids love to have days when there is nothing to do. A subpar beach town with lousy weather doesn't bother a kid at all. Incorporate do-nothing days — or at least afternoons — into your itinerary from the start or it'll be tempting to cram in another sight to see.

KIDS LOVE TO HAVE DAYS WHEN THERE IS NOTHING TO DO

3 **Hobbies/interests.** One parent found success in integrating her teen's current hobby — scootering — into the itinerary. She researched their destination and found a skatepark in every town they were planning to visit. Another smart mom promised her daughters "a playground a day" on their European vacation. When kids can expect some time to have their fun, they are more tolerant of "adult" activities that would normally inspire whining.

4 **Hall passes.** Plan to let your kids skip some activities. Maybe the tweens/teens can stay in the hotel alone. Or maybe the parents can tag-team and take a solo afternoon/day to do their own thing. Or maybe you hire a local sitter. Freedom begets peace.

YOUR GUIDE TO BETTER PICS

One look through ROAM's gallery of Best Family Travel Photos and it hit me: I gotta take better vacation photos! Luckily, ROAM's winners were happy to share their expertise. The bottom line? Take a ton of pictures. Don't pose. And a phone camera might be all you need to pack.

Shoot memories. While traveling, the purpose of your photography shouldn't simply be getting a classic picture of your kids with the Eiffel Tower or Taj Majal — you won't forget visiting the famous spots. Instead, take pictures of yourselves in unique locations or with things that trigger your best memories of the trip.

Take tons. It never fails that in any given picture, one kid is smiling beautifully while the other is blinking or mid-sneeze. Get around this by having lots of shots to choose from later.

Be social. Be as social as possible with the locals. You'll end up in situations where you can quickly take out the camera for a couple of shots.

Get down. Drop to the level of your kids' eyes for a unique perspective.

Go quickly. When kids are traveling they are anxious, tired, or curious, and you can't hold their attention for very long. Forget posing or waiting for the perfect shot and just shoot!

Use video. When trying to get a shot of wildlife, action or anything else that's unpredictable and fast, begin shooting a video. You'll be able to do a screen grab later of the exact spot that monkey jumps to the next tree.

Let the kids play. Let your children take photos too, they have a different perspective and a fun take on what makes for a great shot.

Fix it later. So much is always going on in a family shot that it is important to draw the viewer's eye to what you're really trying to show. Learn a simple app like PicMonkey to crop those pics after the fact.

FORGET POSING OR WAITING FOR THE PERFECT SHOT AND JUST SHOOT

TECH

25 MUST-HAVE APPS

Before I book in or pack up, I load down my phone with the latest versions of all my favorite travel apps. Here are the ones I can't or won't leave home without.

Kayak, Skyscanner and **Hopper** are my faves for booking flights.

SeatGuru helps make sure to pick the best seats on the plane for the entire family.

Rome2rio shows you how best to travel between stops — just plug in where you want to go, and the app will show you options for planes, trains, automobiles, buses and more!

Booking.com to book hotel rooms, **HotelTonight** for last minute rooms and **Airbnb** for a house or loft. I really like Booking.com because all your bookings are stored in one place. You can easily look up your reservations and easily make changes or cancellations. I also trust their verified reviews.

TripAdvisor shows us what activities are available in specific destinations, as well as letting us check reviews on accommodations, tour operators and restaurants. Be sure to click the "family" box to filter reviews and view those written by parents.

Wunderlist allows users to make any type of list. I use it for my trip to-do lists and to set up packing lists for the kids, too.

Mobile Passport is crucial for arrival in the U.S. after international travel. Enter your flight and passport info and skip the hour-long line upon reentry.

LoungeBuddy helps us find access to airport lounges if we end up with long layovers.

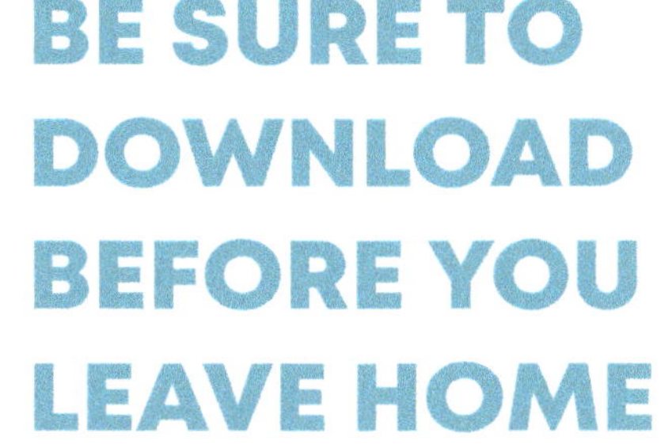

Lyft and **Uber** are money-savers in cities where they operate.

Google Maps If you're going to be offline during the day, be sure to download the local map prior to leaving your hotel wifi zone.

WhatsApp is widely used around the world as a text and communication app, especially when you need to get in touch with a tour operator, Airbnb host or other local and don't have local phone service.

Google Translate is a lifesaver for the random communication challenge with the locals that no phrasebook could see coming.

Currency Converter is my go-to app for keeping tabs on all the money we are spending.

Units Plus comes in handy for converting those pesky American measures into metric ones, and vice versa.

Weather Underground provides updated weather forecasts in an easy-to-use interface.

Yelp (as opposed to TripAdvisor) is what we turn to for restaurant reviews from locals (as opposed to tourists) in areas where Yelp has a large number of users.

Kindle is a must for travelers like me who love to read on vacation. I download a bunch of novels before I leave home so that I'll have enough connectivity to get them onto my phone. I always download a *Lonely Planet* guide for the place we are traveling, too.

Good Eggs (or your local grocery delivery service) is a lifesaver to ensure our refrigerator will be stocked upon arrival with all the foods we missed from home. — *Megan Harvey*

19 ADVENTURES FOR 2019

These trips aren't for every family — and they won't be easy to book this month — or even this year.

ROAM editors' picks for the year's most unique and exciting vacations aim to inspire and shape your family's travel plans for years to come.

COLOMBIA'S
New World

A REBIRTH OF PLAZAS, PLAYAS AND PEOPLE

By Megan Harvey

Our taxi drove for an hour through the night toward what most Americans know as the most dangerous city in the world. Down, down, down through the dark, we wound our way to the bottom of the Aburrá Valley through the struggling outskirts of the city Pablo Escobar's drug empire called home.

But one step into El Poblado's main plaza and we knew Medellín's dark days were gone. The square was alive with Christmas lights, music and people. During our stay, we discovered that not only has the "City of Eternal Spring" been reborn, but the entire country of Colombia. Watching the locals enjoy their cities and parks was inspirational.

We had wanted to spend the entire two weeks of our kids' Christmas holiday break traveling — not just in a different place but really feeling like we were on a long adventure. We wanted a place that could incorporate city, culture, local buses, hostels, villas, hiking, beach time, action and nightlife.

It was a tall order, but we got it all in Colombia — from coffee picking and fishing in the Andes to wandering 500-year-old colonial streets to trekking through rainforest to tropical isles with 50-shades-of-blue water.

One day, after inner-tubing down a river, we found ourselves at a massive beach party in the jungle. It was then that we remembered it was New Year's Eve and we realized we had succeeded in really traveling: Colombia was so engaging that we had lost all sense of date and time. ❖

The ROAM Report
COLOMBIA

✚ **Travelers:** The Harvey Family — Megan, Tom and two kids aged 9 and 13
✚ **Date:** December 2017 & February 2018
✚ **Itinerary:** Two weeks for Medellín, El Jardín, Santa Marta, Tayrona and Cartagena, plus time on Providencia
✚ **Cost:** Approximately $200 per day and night for all expenses (except flights)
✚ **Read more:** bit.ly/roam2019colombia

Medellín

Bike Tour. We celebrated Christmas Day riding with Medellín Bike Tours. Our guide, Dan, had arranged for a smaller bike for our son. He showed us the entire city, which was, luckily, empty of traffic given the holiday. We later explored a huge holiday lights display at a large park with a little lake. The locals were understanding considering we were in bike clothes and they were decked out in nice outfits and fancy shoes.

Metro Ride. The Metro system in Medellín has received global acclaim for connecting all classes of citizens of the city. We rode the Line K, a cable car that connects the once hard-to-reach steep and poor hillside neighborhoods of the main city to the picturesque Parque Arvi, an oasis of nature on the edge of the city.

Coffee Region. We decamped for the colonial pueblo of El Jardín to explore the coffee region and epic vistas of the Andes. We stayed at a little hostel right off the main square. At this point, we really felt like we were traveling. We didn't hear a word of English and most of the other tourists were Colombians.

Jeep Time. We explored the countryside in a Willys jeep and visited a finca with our guide, Wilson. My son loved our next move: a tuk-tuk ride to La Trucheria. He caught trout and the restaurant cleaned and cooked it for us.

Parque Tayrona

Jungle Hike. After checking into our bungalow at the jungle-y Villa Maria, we hiked into the national Parque Tayrona. Visitors have to hike or ride on a horse. The crowds are large and the Caribbean currents are too strong for swimming but the walk is amazing. Take a picnic lunch and skip the packed restaurant.

Tubing Tour. Isn't it funny that so many tours aim for a waterfall? Well, these falls didn't disappoint. We carried inner-tubes with us up the hill and tubed down to the riverside beach where we started. While we were gone, the quiet beach had transformed into a roaring New Year's Eve party! The Colombians know how to do it right.

Providencia

R&R Island. Whatever your route, consider ending your time in Colombia on the paradise of Providencia, a small island off the coast of Nicaragua. The culture is a mix of creole and Colombian. There are no touts on the beach and only a few cars. The island had a solid late lunch scene — don't miss Roland's famous restaurant and reggae bar — but limited dinner options.

Land Exploring. You can circumnavigate Providencia in about 20 minutes but the isle's land packs a lot to see on top. We hiked to the tallest point one day, counting more than 500 lizards on our way up. We rented a 4x4 another day, and drove around the island on our own.

Snorkel Trip. For three of our days on the island, we hired a private boat for $165. Our guide, the fabulous Fabio, took us around the island to a variety of snorkeling spots. The water was fifty shades of blue. Amazing!

Sunset Views. Most accommodations on the island are simple posadas–in fact, there is only one high–end hotel to be found. Sirius, our no–frills hotel on South Bay, had a spot–on view of the sunset and a beautiful beach at our doorstep. Providencia is one of those places you can't wait to get back to and hope it never changes.

Cartagena

Neighborhood Stay. Moving to the 500-year-old north coast port of Cartagena, our base was the up-and-coming neighborhood of Gestsemaní, outside the city walls. We absolutely loved it and our hotel too, Casa Lola. The narrow little streets were lined with cool shops, restaurants and hotels. The walls were covered in graffiti art. The vibe was vibrant with crowds of people gathering outside of the local church to play fútbol during the day and dance and celebrate at night. We explored the walled city at sunset and enjoyed the views.

Boat Trip. We chartered a speed boat through Cartagena Connections for a day exploring the islands off the coast. At the Rosario Islands, we snorkeled, checked out a sunken airplane, and saw the ruins of a former mansion that many claim belonged to a former associate of Pablo Escobar. Later, we got some beach time on the tiny coves around Isla Barú and on a quick visit to Colombia's always-spring-break party scene of Cholón.

PERFECT TIME

GLACIAL ACTION AND LEGENDARY HIKING IN ARGENTINA'S SOUTH

By Sarah Hart

"The bridge will come down at any moment!!!" the clerk yelled as we neared the front desk.

We had no idea what he was talking about. We had just made our way through the billowing white curtains into the hotel's monastery-meets-spa, Enya-blaring lobby, my husband and I nodding to each other that we'd chosen the wrong hotel for our energetic kids.

But this man was emphatic.

"Everyone is at the glacier — GO!" the clerk demanded, gesturing wildly.

We had suspected something was up from the moment we landed that morning. We remembered how the tiny local airport had been brimming with travelers and excitement. And many tourists were weighed down by super fancy cameras and gear — but we'd landed in southern Patagonia and assumed everyone comes prepped for a once-in-a-lifetime experience.

We didn't know if we should be excited or afraid, but even the kids knew he was serious. We threw caution to the wind, jumped back in the car and headed for the glacier. As my husband headed down the highway and the kids bubbled with anticipation in the backseat, I braved the spotty wireless to figure out what was going on.

Perito Moreno is the most famous of Argentine glaciers. Once every few years, huge chunks of ice begin dropping into the lake below, resulting in the collapse of a massive ice "bridge" connecting the glacier to the mainland. Scientists, photographers, tourists, and locals wait up to 15 years for the chance to see the natural spectacle — but our luck landed us in the hottest spot in icy Patagonia at precisely the perfect moment.

The drive from our hotel to the glacier was about 40 miles, and we were making good time until a heavy, icy rain began to fall. As we got closer to the park, the traffic became stop and go. After waiting in traffic for almost two hours, a bunch of cars started streaming

The ROAM Report

SOUTHERN PATAGONIA, ARGENTINA

✚ **Travelers:** Two adults and two kids, ages 7 and 10.
✚ **Dates:** One week in spring 2018, as part of a three-month sabbatical
✚ **Itinerary:** El Calafate (1 night, then 2 additional nights upon return from El Chaltén) and El Chaltén (4 nights).
✚ **Cost:** $1,500 (excluding flights)
✚ **Read more:** bit.ly/roam2019/patagonia

toward us, leaving the park. We assumed we had missed the big event but decided to keep on going, hoping we could at least get a glimpse of the glacier while we were there.

By the time we parked and rode the bus to the entrance, it was nearly 5 p.m. and storm clouds were gathering. We grabbed some warm cookies and tea at the snack bar, headed out over the catwalks, and got our first glimpse of big ice.

We were completely awed by the massive blue slab — but we continued to hurry down the path to the viewing platform. To our surprise, the bridge was still there!

The rain had thinned the crowds so we were able to squeeze ourselves into a good viewing spot. We spent the next two hours mesmerized. Every time a chunk of ice would crash spectacularly into the water, the crowd would erupt in cheers and we would happily join them.

As night began to fall and the storm became more intense, officials closed the park and shuttled all of the disappointed guests back to their cars without seeing the big finale. But we were actually the last group to see the bridge intact: That sneaky arch collapsed later, in the dark, with only a few park rangers in attendance.

We didn't care that we had missed the actual collapse; our family had witnessed something truly remarkable that we would never forget. We drove away buzzing with excitement, so grateful for what we had seen, and completely blown away by our first glimpse of the enormity and expansiveness that is Patagonia. ❖

THE GOOD STUFF
The El Calafate Area

Glaciers Galore. If Perito Moreno isn't enough for you, there's a ton of companies offering half-day and full-day boat tours to see others: Upsala (the largest in South America) and Spegazzini.

Glaciarium. This super cool, modern museum focuses on glaciers and on the terrain of southern Patagonia, featuring interactive exhibits, short films, and everything you have ever wanted to know about snow and ice. The location is incredible.

Ice Bar. The most exciting part of the Glaciarium for my kids was the 20 minutes we spent in its Ice Bar. For an additional fee, we were led down some stairs into the basement of the museum and outfitted in shiny superhero capes, gloves, and boots, all designed to keep us from getting hypothermia. We were offered ice glasses of Sprite and vodka and invited to dance around to blaring techno, which of course we did.

Laguna Nimez. Glaciered out? This ecological reserve has 80 different types of birds, including the Chilean flamingo, and it is a great kid hike.

Lodging. The Santa Monica Aparts are clean, quiet and well-situated. They were so helpful and friendly, and delivered warm croissant-like medialunas, coffee, tea, and fruit every morning.

Food. El Calafate is a decently large town so we found some good meals while we were there. Las Cruces was perfect for kids and the food at La Zeina and Mi Rancho was excellent, especially if you like steak and your littles are able to chill out for a sit-down meal.

The Big Trek

We had decided early on that we would hike as far as seemed doable, then turn around and head back when our 7-year-old started to wilt — possibly to the 4 km turning point which has a fabulous view of the Fitz Roy peaks. Fueled by other trekkers, and a shameless Starburst candy bribe at every kilometer sign, the kids exceeded our expectations. Up until the very end of the hike, the trail was completely manageable, but there's an abrupt grade change in the last kilometer as you climb a narrow trail on crumbly rock. My kids were in, but several adults, coming down, some nearly in tears, said it was very icy and slippery and that the conditions seemed to be worsening; in short, head back. Although we were a bit disappointed, it ended up being the right choice. By the time we returned to town, we had hiked about 14 miles over 8 hours and my little one's feet were pretty sore. Still, we were proud we'd made it so far and were dazzled by all we had seen.

The El Chaltén Area

Ski Town Vibe. Considered the trekking capital of Argentina, El Chaltén is a small village surrounded by the Fitz Roy and Cerro Torre Mountains. Similar to a low key ski town, this village really exists because of all the trekkers and climbers who are drawn to the area. We spent 4 nights in this awesome little village and could have easily stayed longer. We had fantastic, cozy dinners at La Cerveceria Artesanal and La Tapera.

The Hiking! This is why you come to Patagonia: Unbelievable hiking trails with beautiful vistas at every turn. We did three hikes over three days, sadly forfeiting our fourth day because of inclement weather.

1. Mirador de Los Condores proved to be a great afternoon hike.
2. Chorillo del Salto was a very short hike to a gorgeous waterfall.
3. Sendero al Fitz Roy is the most famous hike in the region.

Post-Hike Treats. After a long day of hiking in cold wet weather, there's nothing quite like a stop at La Waffleria, a super cozy spot with choose-your-own-topping waffles. Pair with a *submarino* (do-it-yourself hot chocolate served as hot milk with a chocolate bar) and all whining comes to a halt and you are ready for a nap. Thank you, gods of sugar and bribery.

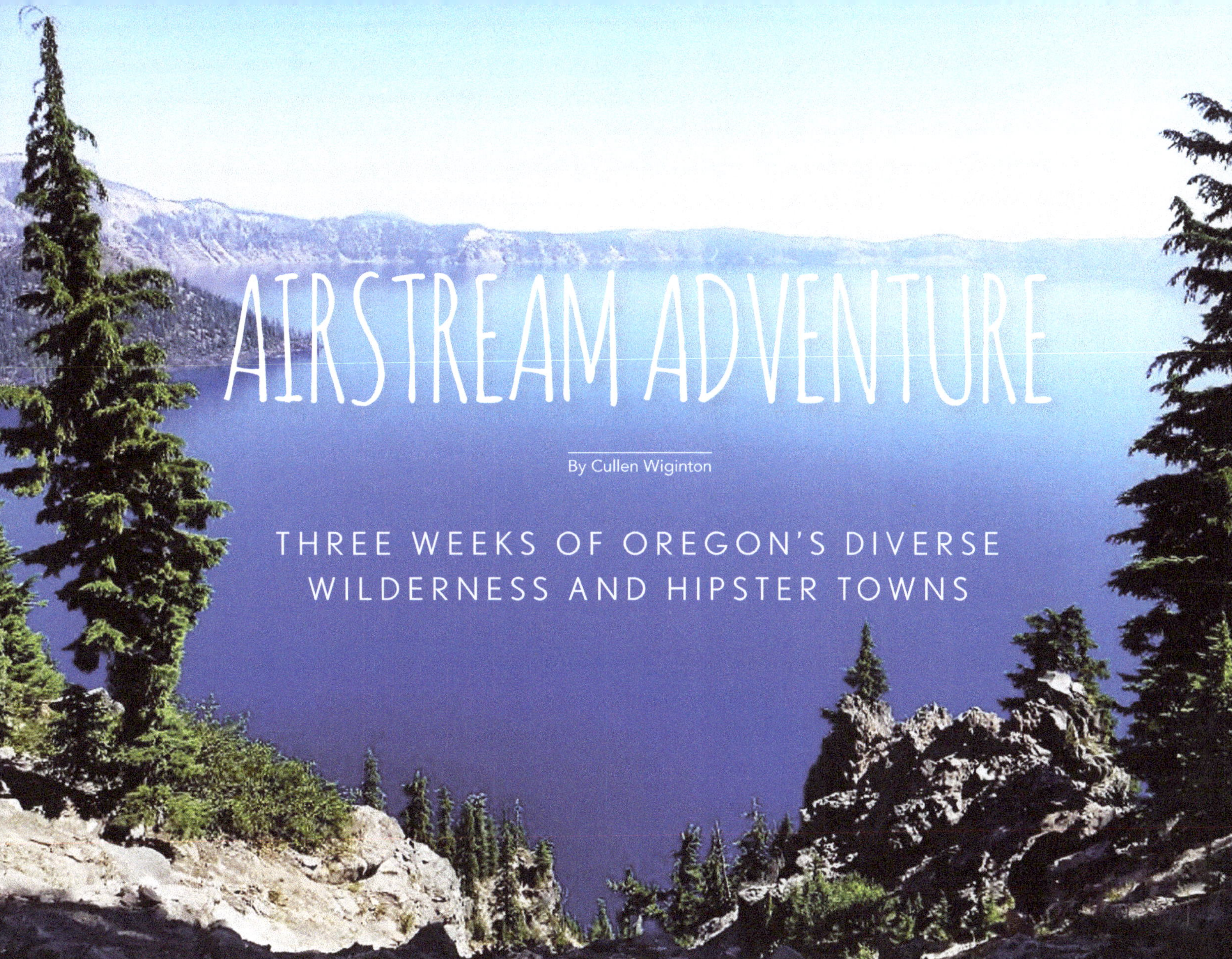

As we approached an extended climb up Highway 97 in far northern California, it hit me: "What did we get ourselves into?" Our 18-year-old Toyota SUV had never failed before, but we had also never asked her to pull a carload of four and a 5,700-pound Airstream up a mountain pass. She was doing her best, but our RPMs were rising as fast as our speed was dropping. Slowly, we sputtered up the incline as a line of traffic backed up behind us on the two-lane road. My hands were death-gripped around the steering wheel.

"Are you leaning forward?" my wife asked with a smile, as she looked judgingly at my driving posture.

"Yes," I replied. "Do you think it is helping?"

While perching at the front of my seat actually did little to help, we ultimately made it over the crest and began our descent toward the Oregon border and our three-week trailer camping adventure: Engine sputters, a knotted muscle between my shoulder blades, and a fair amount of evil eyes from the few lucky drivers who were able to pass our giant rig. My shot nerves made me wonder if our inaugural trip might also be our last.

Were we really trailer people? Just weeks before, we had purchased a used Airstream trailer as a part of an extended midlife crisis that has been playing out in our family; we were excited to see where "Rusty, the Big Gray Whale" would take us. A big part of this crisis involved my wife and I busily concocting crazy travel schemes, while our pragmatic kids rolled their eyes at each new plan, understanding that any efforts to dissuade us were futile.

But our Airstream scheme was a big hit. We zigzagged the best of the Beaver State — from hiking near cobalt Crater Lake to inner-tubing in Sunriver to sipping "craft everything" in Bend to berry picking in the Columbia River Gorge. We watched lumberjacks "log roll" and tasted "hipster everything" in Portland before moving to the epic vistas of the coast, where the seafood,

beach walks, dune rolls, whale watching, and small-town marinas provided nonstop entertainment — not to mention a chance to master the "22-point U-turn."

"Are you driving with one hand?!?" my wife asked in shock and awe as I deftly navigated coastal turns. I'm not sure what let me shed my ball of nerves, but by the time we neared the California border again on our ride home, I had found my happy place. We were no longer hurrying to get anywhere; we were enjoying the ride. Because after 21 days and 2,000 miles Airstreaming around Oregon, I came to a realization: Indeed, we are now trailer people. ❖

OREGON BY AIRSTREAM

+ **Travelers:** Cully, Jan, and the kids 9 and 7, plus our trailer dubbed "Rusty, the Big Gray Whale"
+ **Date:** August 2018
+ **Itinerary:** Seven days up through central California and Oregon, five days in Portland and the Columbia River Gorge and nine days working our way down the coast back home.
+ **Cost:** About $50 a night average for our camping spots. Approximately $800 for gas. $50 to $200 per day for food and activities, depending on whether eating in or dining out.
+ **Read more:** bit.ly/roam2019oregon

THE GOOD STUFF

Crater Lake

What a sight Crater Lake is to behold: The view from the rim, hundreds of feet above the lake, is amazing, with vibrant blues and greens; it's seemingly the most pristine body of water we'd ever seen. A leisurely hike on the Discovery Point Trail near the visitor center is wide, flat and perfect for families (though you'll want to grab a hand for some of the cliffside spots.)

Cleetwood Cove is the one point where you can get down to water level for a swim in Crater Lake. It is accessed by a steep trail that descends over 700 feet from the parking lot. The trip down to the lake was easy enough, and we were rewarded with crystal clear water, which was a chilly 55 degrees, but a welcome refresher on a hot day. The way back up? A little complain-y. The steep uphill trail was a tough one in the heat of the day, and our kids definitely could have used a donkey or a sherpa. A stop by the visitor center for some ice cream made everyone feel better.

Sunriver/Bend

Much like their big-city counterparts in Portland, Bend's hipster locals revel in good food, creative spaces, and "craft" everything. This was on full display at Spoken Moto — a motorcycle shop that included several food trucks, a coffee shop, a craft beer bar, and a clothing boutique.

A trip to Bend isn't complete without getting in the Deschutes River. While renting tubes from Tumalo Creek Kayak & Canoe, we happened to run into some old friends, and formed a giant flotilla. Even in August the water was a bit chilly, but floating the river was a ton of fun.

The Coast

The Cannon Beach Hardware & Public House is a unique restaurant/hardware store combination that lets you dine next to a large display of screws and bolts. Where else can you get fish and chips and a coax cable under the same roof?! The famed Haystack Rock on Cannon Beach is impressive in size and a true natural wonder, jutting out of the surf and into the salty air.

And who could resist a dune buggy excursion with Sandland Tours? More roller-coaster ride than day tour, the zooming experience was an incredibly fun way to explore the dunes while getting a rush of adrenaline.

The gorgeous bluff-top setting made Harris Beach State Park another of our most memorable spots to stay. Our kids made friends at the large playground, and we enjoyed a hike down to the coast to spend a little time at the beach.

Columbia River Gorge

The Columbia River Gorge area has a lot to offer. We watched windsurfers, hiked up the short but steep Beacon Rock Trail for breathtaking views of the valley, and visited the impressively high cascade of Multnomah Falls.

Dining-wise, a can't-miss stop on a trip through the valley is the Brigham Fish Market. From their outdoor tables overlooking the river, we enjoyed amazing local smoked salmon chowder and sturgeon fish and chips before picking blackberries off the bushes outside for dessert.

Portland

After checking into the Sandy Riverfront RV Resort and enjoying an afternoon swim, we played some laid-back golf and ate an al fresco dinner while exploring the sprawling Edgefield McMenamins. The hard-to-describe hotel compound that revitalized the property of a poor house from the early 1900s and incorporates restaurants, bars, a winery, a brewery, a movie theater, and a very short par-3 style golf course.

We took the kids to many family-friendly foodie spots downtown. From the outstanding brunch at Tasty N Alder, to the Thai street food at Pok Pok, to the stops for sweets at Voodoo Donuts and Salt and Straw, the eating in Portland did not disappoint.

GO LOCAL

We loved sampling the local goods everywhere we went. Coffee from local roasters in Portland, ice cream from Tillamook, locally caught seafood in the Columbia River Gorge. And let's not forget the beer. It seems even the smallest towns in Oregon had at least one craft brewery.

GO SLOW

Packing up every day doesn't let you stop to smell the roses. We tried to stay at least two nights in every spot so we could explore the area, and realized that many of the gems we discovered were during that one extra day.

GO GOURMET

Just because you're camping doesn't mean you have to eat hot dogs and beans every day. I love to cook, and the combination of a real (albeit, small) kitchen in the trailer, Oregon local foods, and being on "vacation time" meant some pretty tasty meals on the road.

CAMBODIA
WAY MORE THAN ANGKOR

GO LOCAL IN KEP AND OTHER STILL-KHMER SPOTS

By Maryann Jones Thompson

"Sleepy little fishing village... Nothing to do... Good crab." One read of *Lonely Planet's* description and Kris Warner was making a beeline for Kep. The former French colonial resort on Cambodia's southeast coast has grown considerably since that first visit in 2005 – and so has Warner's footprint there. Together with his wife, Naome, the Californian founded Khmer Hands, a non-profit vocational and arts school.

The school runs a guest house, restaurant, café and store, and trains underprivileged locals for jobs in the region's burgeoning tourist industry.

Families and backpackers from around the world use Khmer Hands as a friendly, budget base to explore the still-authentic seaside town only a dozen miles from the Vietnamese border. Kep has a bustling crab market, with cafes serving heaps of the steamed critters and towers of cold Angkor beer. From the town beach, you can see Rabbit Island, where old-school Southeast Asian-style bungalows on the sand can still be found. Trails through the Kep National Park run just above town, with towering bamboo and ocean views. And many more untouristed sites like the caves and grottos of Kampong Trach are just a moto-ride away – if you can stand riding your kids on the back or letting your teens ride alone.

Just one big town to the west, Kampot also draws Cambodia's off-the-beaten-track set. You can see both salt and pepper farms, including the must-tour Sothy's. There is rock climbing, SUP-ing, caving, boating and more hiking to the Bokor Hill Station. Or just wander the still small-town streets, hit a festival, and bask in the local scene. But go soon because big change comes fast in this small country: Cambodia drew 6.2 million tourists in 2018, up from just 1 million in 2004, which makes genuine small-town Khmer life harder and harder to find. ❖

The ROAM Report

KEP, CAMBODIA

+ **Travelers:** Maryann and Don Thompson, plus 2 teens
+ **Date:** January 2017
+ **Itinerary:** Stayed five nights at Khmer Hands in Kep as part of a three-week trip in Cambodia.
+ **Cost:** Bungalows at Khmer Hands cost under $40 per night
+ **Read more:** bit.ly/roam2019cambodia

THE GOOD STUFF

Your family time will start by landing at Sihanoukville or Phnom Penh airport and arranging a car to drive your family to one of these less-touristed Cambodian classics.

Waterfalls in Tatai

Your bungalow steps descend straight into the water at the tiny Tatai Riverfront Lodge. Day trips cruise you to waterfalls for jumping, swimming and eating.

Sands of Lazy Beach

These bungalows lie on the quiet side of Koh Rong Samloem and serve the perfect splashy waves, simple huts in the sand and elaborate meals in the restaurant.

Elephants in Sen Monorom

The Elephant Valley Project wrote the book on responsible elephant tourism. Your hands-on work and tourist dollars help preserve the sanctuary and health of their retired captive ellies.

Dolphins in Kratie

This Mekong River village features camping and kayak paddles to see the endangered Irrawaddy dolphins.

Trekking in the Cardamoms

A super rustic homestay program in Chi Phat will show you rural life and help "re-wild" its forests.

Streets of Phnom Penh

We can't stay in Cambodia without a stay at the Kabiki, a lounge on its porch, and a dip in its green pool. The location is perfect for wandering the tree-lined streets and getting a glimpse of the bustling central city.

ANOTHER TASTE OF
San Sebastián

SPAIN'S GO-BACK-TO-BASQUE BEACH TOWN

By Dina Harrison

With all the fascinating corners of the world left to explore, a place has to be pretty incredible for me to visit twice in two years. San Sebastián is that incredible.

Sure, there are some sights to see. But it's the magnetic Basque lifestyle, food, and culture that attracts us to the northern Spanish town on the Bay of Biscay. We spend long, lazy days at the beach and love to stroll the New Paseo along the curve of Playa de la Concha with its hallmark white railing.

The *donostiarras* — the people of Donostia, San Sebastián's Basque name — create some of the world's best cuisine. You can wander the streets and drop in hundreds of *pintxos* bars for evening "happy hour," enjoying the Basque tapas with a glass of local *txakoli* (white sparkling wine) or beer with the kids. Rest up and head out later for a more formal dinner at one of the town's Michelin-starred restaurants, or just wander the streets for sweets and boutiques, hang out just outside of Parte Vieja, listen to music, people watch, or take another walk on the Paseo. It's very addictive. ❖

Stay at the beach

The best place to stay is near La Concha or near Parte Vieja. You can also stay near Zurriola Beach and be walking distance to almost everything.

Paseo some time

Walk or bike the New Paseo, which starts (or ends) at Zurriola beach and ends (or starts) at the beach of Ondarreta. You walk all along the sea — including Playa la Concha — and get great people watching, beautiful sights, and Instagram-worthy photos at every turn.

The ROAM Report

SAN SEBASTIÁN, SPAIN

✛ **Travelers**: Dina & Steve Harrison with two kids, aged 7 to 10
✛ **When:** July 2017 and July 2018
✛ **Itinerary:** 4–6 nights in San Sebastián and 1 night Bilbao
✛ **Cost:** The suites and the apartment are each about $300–$600/night, depending on the time of year and how big of a place you need.
✛ **Read more:** bit.ly/roam2019sansebastian

Get high

Hike, walk, or take the funicular to the top of Mount Igueldo. The views of La Concha and the city of San Sebastián are incredible. There's a small old-timey amusement park for kids and a really old and slightly scary roller coaster.

Go fish

Walk the path up Mount Urgull. This is a great way to stretch your legs in the morning and see the park. It's in the old part of town and at the base is the aquarium. My kids love all things fish- and sea-related, and the aquarium is a nice way to beat the heat for a couple of hours.

Shop small

Shopping the boutiques in Gros and in San Sebastián is also a nice way to spend some time — and money! We liked how many mom-and-pop boutiques are mixed in with the Spanish giants like Zara and Mango. Our favorite store was Bimba y Lola for their little purses and pouches.

Do a night in Bilbao

My kids were enchanted by photos of the Guggenheim Museum — and well, who am I to say no? Bilbao is a mix of old and new. The museum is the biggest draw in town and afterwards, we headed to Casco Viejo (Bilbao's old town) for sightseeing, restaurants, bars, stores, and churches that kept us busy for hours.

FOOD FOR DAYS

San Sebastián has a global reputation for food, both in fine restaurants and small pintxos bars. In fact, only Kyoto has more Michelin-starred restaurants per square meter than San Sebastián. So if you love good food, you will not go hungry. The kids will enjoy it too — and you won't have to break the bank to try new dishes. San Sebastián has something for everyone at every budget.

PINTXOS BARS

Aim for Parte Vieja and El Barrio de Gros on the other side of the river for our favorite Basque tapas spots:

Bar Nestor for steak — well, all they serve is steak — egg pancakes, tomatoes, and peppers, so you know they do them all well
Bar Sport for their foie gras (heavenly!)
Ganbara for their mushrooms
Goiz Argi for their garlic prawn skewers (hands-down favorite), but also their ropa vieja
La Cepa for ham and cheese sandwiches
La Vina for cheesecake (if you have room after all the pintxos)
Paco Bueno for fried shrimp
Txepetxa for anchovies
Bar Bergara is a classic pintxos bar and one of our favorites.
Aitzgorri is a great spot for a bigger meal, they serve seasonal food and speak some English

MICHELIN-STARRED RESTAURANTS

For fine dining, there are plenty of gastro notables in the area, including the Michelin three-star winners like Akelarre, Arzak, Martín Berasategui, and two-starred Mugaritz. We loved late lunch at Rekondo on the outside terrace. There are also plenty of one-star places, including Alameda, Amelia, Elkano, Eme Be Garrote, Kokotxa, Mirador de Ulia, and Zuberoa. Be sure to reserve your table well in advance for summer meals — and if you can't get a spot for dinner, do lunch!

Venture nearby

San Sebastián is very close to the French border. In fact, it's only about 30 miles from Biarritz in France. You are also 200 miles to Picos de Europa, a national park with fantastic hiking and sightseeing. Another cool spot is the fairly new Hotel Marqués de Riscal, designed by Frank Gehry. If I weren't with the kids, this luxury hotel complete with spa, wine tasting and yes, more delicious Basque cuisine, would be an ideal night–or–two jaunt.

MANTA-HUNTING

ON YAP

By Maryann Jones Thompson

The manta rays have names in Yap. This is Fumiko.

While some divers scour the seven seas in search of the big beauties, manta sightings in Yap are virtually guaranteed — it is just a matter of how many and which ones you will meet. In the mating season from December to May, trains of mantas dance around the main island of this Micronesian state, a 90 minute flight southwest of Guam.

But in summer, when we visited, there is a bit more luck and patience involved. After splashing down into a surging current, we maneuvered ourselves to the base of a coral head known to be a cleaning station and hung out for nearly an hour, hoping a manta would stop by.

Sitting still anywhere is tough for any kid — or adult — these days. You start to sift through grains of sand. You watch a single fish nose around a rock. Then another. Then you see something big move out of the corner of your eye: It's your teenage son changing positions, kicking up sand, clearing his mask, making bubble rings with his fists. Your guide motions to him, "Settle down." The settling down lasts for a few moments before the twitching resumes. Ugh.

Luckily, Fumiko must have been desperate for a good bath. She swooped in right as we were about to give up and head to the surface. She hovered above us like a UFO for a good ten minutes of all-over nibbles from cleaner wrasse. And boy, did she know how to settle down my teenager — and quick. It was the first dive in a week of finding mantas, tornados of barracuda, swarms of sharks, macro critters and picturesque swim-throughs.

Yap proved to be one of the most curious and compelling islands we've ever visited. As a former U.S. protectorate, the Yapese speak English like they're from The O.C. But the island's traditions are straight out of a decades-old *National Geographic* cover story with beautiful islanders, hand-built dwellings, stone money, and secret ceremonies. Nearly 6,500 miles from the California coast, Yap is much closer to Papua New Guinea and the Philippines. Aside from divers, not too many tourists make the long journey. In fact, the largest number of foreigners to arrive onshore were the

Japanese during WWII. Tourists can see eerie wreckage of planes and ships that have been left for nature to devour-like *Lost* come to life.

Originally from Texas, Bill Acker arrived on Yap with the Peace Corps in the 1970s, worked on the island after grad school, married Patricia, and developed manta ray diving. He founded Yap Divers and then the Manta Ray Resort, and can still be found chatting with guests on the top deck of the *Mnuw*, an Indonesian schooner docked out front that serves as a bar and restaurant with fresh poke to die for.

Planes come and go only a few times per week and do so smack in the middle of the night — no joke — at like 2 a.m. or 4 a.m. When you arrive to the tiny terminal, a local girl drapes a homemade flower lei around your neck. It is still legitimately traditional — like visiting Hawaii a hundred years ago. You can't really buy souvenirs or plan to see any Yapese ceremonies or faux dancing, but if you're lucky to be there for a genuine display like we were, Manta Ray will shuttle you to the village to watch it.

The dance we attended was performed by the men of the village. When we pulled up, there were moms sitting in groups at the edge of the performance area, fussing over the headdress feathers, loin cloth placements and bronzing oils applied to their young sons, just like a dance or soccer mom back in the U.S. The elder men were dressed equally exotically and led the boys into a clearing to perform a series of dances

Good to Know

A Sort-of Resort. Manta Ray provides everything you need in one convenient spot — a dive shop and marina, restaurant, plunge pool and room. There aren't any sprawling Hawaiian resort-type grounds — but you won't miss them.

Kid-Friendly Care. For parents with little non-divers, Manta coordinates babysitting and village outings.

Flying In. With United miles, we hopped from the U.S. to northeast Asia (we flew SFO to Seoul), then to Palau for a week, then continued to Yap. On the way home, we flew to Guam then SFO, but many travelers connect via Hawaii as well.

and chants. Local spectators videoed with iPads and cameras, and then topped their heads with banana leaves when a light rain began to fall.

After the performance, the chief approached us and we nodded and smiled in appreciation, unsure of his English capabilities. He took his crown of fresh flowers, placed it on my daughter's head, and spoke with the slight Midwestern twang of my Grandpa Jones, "Darn this climate change. It's not supposed to rain this time of year." ❖

By Jennifer & Dennis Harrison

TREKKING WITH THE WOMEN OF LADAKH

HIMALAYAN VETERANS AIM FOR INDIA'S KONZKE LA

We had just hit 14,000 feet when the unimaginable happened. We were pushing for our highest pass after a plane, a bus, and three days of walking. We had worried about a twisted ankle, an intractable kid, a bout of stomach or altitude sickness, and, most obviously, a slip and fall, but we did not foresee the most vexing problem that would befall our trek.

We had always wanted to trek in Ladakh. East of Pakistan and south of China, north of the Himalayas and south of the Karakorums, trekkers descend on the Indian region in the summer and head into the mountains along ancient trading routes. But picking a guide and a route from halfway around the world hadn't been easy.

"Ladhaki Women's Travel Company" came up often in our research, but the outfitter was obviously local and small; its web site was old and only had a few reviews. But after interacting with several tour guides, LWTC was the only one that could deliver a custom, off-track experience and be flexible enough to work with our family.

The outfitter is run entirely by women — even the porters in training to be guides — which we loved. They specialize in homestays in the remote villages. Because the men of Ladakh often leave the village for work, the women stay behind to tend the fields and care for the family. The LWTC puts real money in the pockets of the locals — and who better to watch over our family than the women who raised their own kids in the mountains?

We'd actually asked for a tough trek. One that would push us — but not too far. We had trekked the Annapurna Sanctuary with our kids a few years ago, so we thought we had an idea of what to expect. In the end, we decided on a remote route — an 8-day journey away from the touristed tracks and into the Sham region — one that would cross several passes, including one upward of 16,000 and one above 17,000 feet.

LANDING IN LEH

"It's like a planet out of Star Wars," our 15-year-old daughter said when we landed in Leh, Ladakh's capital, and laid eyes on the barren alpine landscape. It was nothing like the rest of India at all. It reminded us of an exaggerated version of California's eastern Sierra Nevadas, a place we go mountain biking every summer.

We had skipped the notoriously harrowing 33-hour bus ride and flew direct from Delhi. Leh's patchwork of green barley and vegetable fields stood out against the bone-dry hills. Most of its 30,000 people are Tibetan Buddhist, but many Kashmiri Muslims call the town home, as well. The streets' mud-brick buildings were striped with prayer flags. The only dodgy thing in town were the street dogs that howled and partied all night.

But a walk across town and up the steps to the King's Palace gave us the first inkling of concern about what we'd signed up for: We were already winded. The magnification of the high-altitude sun... The unquenchable thirst... This trek was not going to be easy.

INTO THE MOUNTAINS

The three Ladakhi women — one guide and two porters — who picked us up, were all pals who had guided together before. Our four-hour drive on hair-raising roads took us along the Indus River and up through the moonscape to 12,000 feet, Lamayuru, the most famous monastery in Ladakh, and the beginning of our trek.

Up we went. Up and up and up. A shepherd passed us heading to his yaks. Then more up and up and up. When we got to the first pass at 12,500 feet after three hours, we felt our first sense of accomplishment. Looking down the other side, the wind gusted across expansive views of 20,000-plus-foot peaks and glaciers.

That night, our homestay had a daughter and son almost exactly the age of our kids, not to mention, lambs!

We slept on mats on the floor, and used the outhouse in the ground-floor stable next to where the livestock live. Life around here hasn't changed much in 500 years — aside from the satellite dishes that top the homes.

Ten minutes of walking on the steep, narrow goat track of Day 2, we were second-guessing our desire to do a tough trek: We were moving in single file for hours, traversing a foot-wide ridge on the side of a gravel slope that headed down below us into a valley for hundreds, if not thousands of feet. If one kid — or anyone, actually — made one wrong step, they would be gone. Maybe the flat paths along the river promised by the other trekking outfits might not have been so bad...

The treacherousness of our situation was completely lost on the kids. They were obliviously chatting with the guides and each other — something that

doesn't happen often at home anymore. But after our son slipped a bit and Dennis (dad) caught him by his pack, Jen (mom) had to move to the front of the line to keep from having an anxiety attack.

Worries swirled as Dennis brought up the rear, keeping one eye on his feet and one eye on his kids. Why did we have to go so big? We should have known better. But it is tough to describe how amazing it felt to be so far out there and to be experiencing this together with our kids. We were the first trekkers of the year to go from Wanla to Urtsi and it felt good to blaze that trail. By the end of the day, everyone was acclimatizing and chit-chatting and feeling much better.

A NEW PATH

Sleeplessly lying on our sleep mats with full bellies of chapati, the nervousness returned: We were heading far higher.

"Really, how tough will the next days be?" Dennis asked the next morning, scanning the map. The women talked amongst themselves in their language for a few minutes. The bottom line? On a scale of 1 to 10, our first few days had been sub-4s, the first pass day would be an 8, and the big pass day would be off-the-charts tough, with knife-like ridges and endless scree.

Uh oh.

We knew we had to trust our guts and be flexible on this journey — and this was go time — or actually, no-go time. Over the protests of our daughter who wanted to stick to our goal, and with the blessings of our son who was up for whatever, we worked with the LWTC to agree on a revised route: Leave most of our gear in the village, head to the 16,240-foot Konzke La pass on a day trek, skip the biggest pass, and complete the trek along more traveled trails. A wave of relief washed over us.

TO THE PASS

The sun and spirits were bright as we headed up and out of the village, beginning our 11-hour day of trekking to the pass. After an hour on the trail, our daughter took a sip of water from her bottle and spurted, "Uh, help…"

Sticking out of her mouth was what looked like a paper clip: A wire had popped off one of the spacers on her braces and was protruding uncomfortably from the side of her lips.

Orthodontia was a challenge the Ladakhi women had not faced. Our porter had an old pair of tiny scissors which proved no match for First World mouth problems. Now what? Our daughter was a trouper, but the broken wire was causing her pain.

The ROAM Report

LADAKH, INDIA

✚ **Travelers:** Jennifer & Dennis Harrison, plus daughter, 15, and son, 12
✚ **Date:** July 2018
✚ **Itinerary:** Three nights pre-trek in Leh, 8-night trek in the Sham region over Khoze La, plus 2 nights post-trek in Leh and a short stay in Dehli afterward
✚ **Cost:** Trek was $1,500 for 4 people
✚ **Read more:** bit.ly/roam2019ladakh

Looking back toward the village to see how far we'd come, we were shocked: A young French couple and their guide were approaching. We hadn't seen a soul on the trail for days! They agreed to help us with the dental crisis. Our daughter laid down in the dirt, Dennis held her mouth open, the Frenchman repeatedly jabbed his Leatherman into her mouth, but the wire was too far back to get ahold of. Eventually, we had to give up and let the couple continue (while taking our hopes of reaching the pass along with them).

But before we could even gather our gear to head down, miraculously, another trekker appeared: A tough old Frenchman walking alone — no guide — with a backpack full of tools. Even luckier? He had once studied to be an orthodontist.

Indeed, the travel gods had been watching over us all along. The second Frenchman snapped the wire in a jiffy and disappeared into the mountains as magically as he had appeared. We never saw another trekker until we reached Khanze La where our son taught the Ladakhi women to "floss" and they taught him a local dance. None of us had ever breathed harder or felt happier. ❖

THE TOUGHEST KILIMANJARO CLIMB

By Elizabeth Weingart

Getting inside a teenager's head is a full-time job — and I've got four. Though all our kids are active, love to play sports, and be outside, if we suggest an afternoon hike in the nearby hills, the answer is "No way." I literally twist arms to get one of my kids to take the dog out for a walk.

But when we throw out the idea of spending seven days of our summer vacation climbing Kilimanjaro — a hike only 40 percent of kids successfully complete? All four are all in.

We'd summited Kilimanjaro before kids. And we'd trekked the Inca Trail as a family. And though our 2018 ascent of Africa's highest peak brought some of us to our knees–literally–we learned we are all at our best when facing a massive challenge. And overcoming one as big as Kili together is something we'll never forget.

The six of us were excited and ready when we set out from our base in Moshi, Tanzania. We had six amazing days on the Lemosho Route, an eight-day path that offers great views and low crowds. Every day was 4–5 hours of challenging hiking but every day was unbelievably beautiful, crossing a variety of terrains on the way up. We would arrive at camp to tents already set up, snacks waiting, and a great evening of talking, card games, music, and fun. Not a screen to be seen.

But as we got higher, it became clear that the peak was still heavy with snow. The guides fessed up that there was far more snow on the ground than they'd seen in a long time. To make matters worse, everyone had packed gym shoes to trek in — except me. When we stopped on the side of the road to buy used boots, our boys' feet were too big, which meant borrowing no-traction footwear from our porters.

As with most summit ascents, we woke at midnight to begin our quest for the peak. From our camp at 15,200 feet, we would aim for the top, Uhuru Peak (19,300 feet), and then descend to camp at 10,100 feet — a total of 13–15 hours to hike 19 kilometers.

Hiking for hours in the cold and dark, I began to feel the first inklings of altitude sickness in my head and stomach. The temperature dipped to -15° Celsius. The water in our Camelbacks was frozen in its tube. Silently I worried: I don't remember it being this cold last time. And I don't remember all this snow. Truly, we

didn't prep the kids for this—and we didn't have gear for it, either.

The going was excruciating — a true test of wills. In the dark, our headlamp illuminated just a few feet in front. We kept thinking the first spot on the peak, Stella Point, was only ten minutes away. But the snowpack meant we were hiking much slower than usual. Not to mention, my kids' feet were literally freezing in their shoes.

My mind raced. "I can't believe we are doing this. Why the heck did we do this?" My head was banging and my nausea increased.

At 6:30 a.m., we finally reached Stella Point. And as excited as we were, we knew we had to get moving because we had another hour to go to reach the top at Uhuru. That's when I got the biggest headache of my life. It was so bad that I couldn't even imagine surviving, descending and saying, "I'm so glad we climbed Kili."

I arrived at Uhuru at 8:30 a.m. and celebrated by throwing up the entire contents of my stomach at the base of the summit sign. All the poor hikers who wanted a photo that day had to stand in my junk. We hugged, high-fived, and shoved chocolate, nuts and mango in our mouths before prepping to do seven-days' worth of ascent in one day of descent.

After returning to sea level, the adventure continued. We spent a week on safari, spending time in the Serengeti for the wildebeest migration and seeing Ngorongoro crater. We followed that with some beach time on Zanzibar, soothing our aching feet in the white sand and crystal water. Our kids were happy to find vacationing European teens to hang out with, and they bonded over Tanzanian adventures and World Cup play.

Looking back, I am so glad we climbed Kili. Day-to-day at home, I know I am blessed with great kids. But watching the four of them persevere to overcome the daunting mental and physical challenges involved with climbing one of the world's Seven Summits, we could not have been prouder. They were truly at their best on Kilimanjaro. We all were. ❖

THE GOOD STUFF

Kilimanjaro Trek

We used Tanzania-based Shah Tours for both the Kilimanjaro trek and the safari. I gave them our budget and they accommodated all our requests. They did a fantastic job from top to bottom. The Lemosho route basically hikes around the mountain as you ascend so we had the crater in our sights nearly the entire time.

Serengeti Safari

After the mountain, we did a six-day safari, following the wildebeest migration for one of the days. We spent one day at Lake Manyara, two days in the Serengeti, two days in Ngorongoro crater and one day at Tarangire. We chose a mid-range trip (as opposed to budget or luxury) and every lodge we stayed at was spectacular. It was so nice that we kept asking ourselves, "If this is mid-range, what does luxury look like?"

Zanzibar Island

To wrap up our Tanzanian adventure, we traveled to Zanzibar and enjoyed some R&R on the west coast in Pongwe at Marafiki Bungalows. The island was gorgeous, with amazing beaches and snorkeling. Stone Town has old cobblestone streets and cool restaurants. We visited the former slave market and the fish market, and we did a spice tour, too. It was the perfect break before our two-day journey home.

Sailing the Coast of Croatia

UNFORGETTABLE FAMILY TIME FROM DUBROVNIK TO THE SOUTHERN DALMATIANS

By Dina Harrison

Floating past the harbors crammed with the faux rich-and-famous, our captain opts for a spot on the back side of the island. The kids and I crane our necks to survey our next stop: A *konoba* (traditional restaurant) surrounded by local boats and sailors. Our captain saunters down the deck and the owner rushes to meet him with a drink and a bear hug.

The kids prepare to restart their routine of jumping and flipping off our catamaran and playing "King of the Hill" on the big unicorn floatie. But wait! The captain has called ahead and arranged bikes for us to ride through the village and into the countryside for a visit to a local winery.

This is yachting in Croatia: A nonstop, Adriatic sea-going parade of unforgettable vistas, splashy games, historical snippets, epic meals, and sunset drinks. Just enjoying each other's company and the beautiful scenery. Bliss!

We teamed up with my brother-in-law's family and chartered a four-bedroom catamaran yacht complete with captain and host. It was a great way to keep us all together, explore the islands without having to choose which one, and sail into coves that you couldn't reach otherwise by land.

Plenty of yachts were from other parts of Europe, but our captain and hostess were both locals from the southern Dalmatians. That meant they could aim for less-crowded harbors and cool off-the-beaten-path locations. Many times, they were personal acquaintances of the konoba owners. They could also speak Croatian, so could call ahead for bikes or other reservations. We had a great relationship with both the captain and the hostess, which made the entire trip go smoothly and provided us with a family trip we'll never forget. ❖

The ROAM Report:

CROATIA

✦ **Travelers:** Dina & Steve Harrison and kids, 9 and 7
✦ **Date:** July 2016
✦ **Itinerary:** 2 weeks in Croatia — 3 nights Dubrovnik, 3 nights Bol, 1 night Split, 7 nights on yacht
✦ **Cost:** The budget can widely vary depending on where you stay in Dubrovnik and Split and the type of boat you rent. High season in July–August is more expensive.

HIGHLIGHTS
FROM THE SOUTHERN DALMATION ISLANDS

- **Paddle boarding** into an old submarine bunker on the island of Vis
- **Seeing the blue cave** of Cave Bisevo off the coast of Split
- **Docking in Vis** and renting scooters and touring the island with the kids on the back
- **Jumping and doing flips** off the boat practically anytime, anywhere
- **Wine** tasting on Komiza
- **Fantastic dinners** on every island, especially Magic Winery on Vis
- **Exploring** the old town of Korcula
- **Eating** at a family farm on Hvar where they grew all the veggies and the father and son caught all the fish. I only wish we knew the name...
- **Watching** all the kids play together, whether it was card games or swimming games

DUBROVNIK WITH KIDS

We began our trip in Dubrovnik and stayed three nights at an apartment outside the city walls. One day was completely devoted to beach time and the others were for exploring, climbing the walls of the city, and seeing the sights. We had long leisurely lunches and enjoyed every minute. We also happened to be in Dubrovnik on days with no cruise ships in port, which was heavenly — much less crowded than what I've heard from others who weren't so lucky. Our top 5 experiences?

- **Cliff jumping at the Buza Bar.** Head over to this hidden-behind-a-gate spot, bring your towel (or not) and lounge and watch all the cliff divers. Even better? Join in on the fun as we did. All different jumps and different heights. Exhilarating!
- **Walking the city walls.** Every time you turn a corner, you'll have a "wow" moment. Between the white marble and the blue, blue sea, every corner is an Instagram moment.
- **Diving into seafood.** We loved our lunch outside the city walls at both Restaurant Posat and Dubrovka 1836.
- **Heading out to a beach club.** We liked our little hike over to Sveti Jacobi (Saint Jacob) beach. Note that the beaches are more pebbly than sandy and your kids may want water shoes!
- **Watching the sunset.** Never gets old in Croatia!

TIPS FOR CHARTERING A YACHT IN CROATIA

- Decide if you need a captain AND a host — the person who cleans upand cooks.
- Determine what size boat you need — how many bedrooms and conveniences.
- If you are prone to seasickness (as I can be), consider a catamaran. Cats are less wobbly because of the dual pontoons.
- Find a reputable charter company — there are many to choose from. We used Angelina Charters and were happy with their service.
- Determine where you'd like to go on the boat, but keep an open mind. The captains know more about what's best. We wanted to go to both the Hvar area and the Kornati Islands, but they are really far apart. This would have meant too much time sailing from Point A to Point B and then back, more money for gas and less water time for the kids.
- Figure out who's paying for gas (usually the customer).
- Determine if you need extras on board. We had a giant unicorn floatie, which we all loved. We also had two paddleboards, which we used a decent amount.
- Do research or ask questions to try to get a great captain. A lot of the boat experience comes down to the captain. We had a great team and it made for a great trip.

Rafting Heaven
in Hell's Canyon

By Don Thompson

My non-fishing son was hooked. "I got six!" he shouted in that elevated voice teenagers use when they are actually ecstatic but have to hide their excitement to remain cool. In the hour between pulling our rafts out of the Snake River and hearing the dinner bell clang, my son had pulled out a half dozen smallmouth bass — many nearing 18 inches long.

The kid who couldn't tie on a lure 48 hours before had become a fishing freak. Over our four-day, father-son trip with America's Rafting Company in Hell's Canyon, on the Snake River bordering Oregon and Idaho, my son caught so many fish that we lost count. He fished from the raft; he fished from the rocks; he fished before breakfast; he fished before bed.

And then there was the rafting.

The Snake River actually "snakes" back and forth through the canyon for 34 miles. The water could look deceptively mellow but definitely delivered big river thrills. Our guides would often walk us up on a bluff to scout upcoming rapids and recommend strategies.

The trip encounters several stretches of Class III and IV drop pool rapids — big water followed by calm pools — which results in roller coaster–level fun. (They often felt like hitting the bottom of the drops on the Pirates of the Caribbean ride at Disneyland.)

ARC also brings inflatable kayaks for guests to use. As soon as my son realized that was an option, he spent as much time as possible in the kayak — even flipping twice in Class IV rapids. For a teenager, the flips were utter bliss.

My favorite meal is always breakfast, and this trip did not disappoint: Huevos rancheros, biscuits, and gravy, eggs with potato hash and banana-bread french toast. Hot coffee, yogurt, and homemade granola were always at the ready. We were constantly stuffed.

After a big breakfast, each day began with a few hours on the water, a lunch stop, then a few more hours before stopping to camp around 4 p.m. There was plenty of time to relax, hike around, fish, catch up with fellow rafters, and play cards, bocce or horseshoes — more items magically pulled from the perfectly-packed gear boat.

Hell's Canyon made for a ruggedly handsome backdrop to the Snake's wet wildness. Its craggy peaks give way to golden grasses and scrub trees as land meets river. We watched deer sneak down for a sip from the river and bighorn graze on the beach.

Our group stopped to hike to vista points, see Native American petroglyphs and visit old homesteads with long-abandoned plum trees, farm equipment, and hand-hewn log cabins.

At night, the sky exploded with a snake of stars framed by the black walls of the canyon. This was especially true at our Oregon Hole camp where even though the canyon was very narrow, somehow, the Milky Way lined up perfectly in the gap. My son slept outside the tent but with such a comfy setup, I usually ended up inside before falling asleep. The only bit of nature we missed were the mosquitos: rolling rivers gather no biters.

Our favorite night was actually the last one. After days of catch and release, Lauren promised she would cook up our Day 3 catch during dinner. The afternoon's rapids and scenery were lost on my son: He spent all day with his line in the water, snagging 10 for dinner. Lauren dusted the filets in spiced cornmeal and then lightly fried them to perfection. My son pronounced it "the best fish ever." And I agreed. ❖

Lauren Duggan and Jarrett von Jess took over America's Rafting Company three years ago, arriving in Idaho via Jackson Hole where they ran a catering company.

The union produced an expert and delicious expedition — but what do you expect when a chef and a rafting guide team up?

Out of the Dutch ovens came rosemary beer bread, blue cornbread, chocolate zucchini cake, and s'mores pie. Pork loin, tri-tip, and chicken exited the grill and met home-canned jalapeño pickles, honey mustard, and salsa verde. Fresh salads and fruits were served at every meal. Drinks emerged from a cooler stocked with soft drinks, wine, and interesting local microbrews. And, of course, happy hour brought a daily cocktail with appetizers before dinner even started. It was like I was eating at the farmers' market rather than a day's float from the nearest road.

This stretch of the Snake River remains inaccessible to cars and day visitors, which helps explain the fantastic fishing.

We had riverside campsites to ourselves — after the bighorn sheep, deer, and chukar partridges moved along, of course. Bald eagles perched in pairs on the cliffs near the river. We saw few other rafts and heard only the rush of the Snake — except when the occasional jet boat tour zoomed past.

GOING WILD FOR SOUTH AFRICA SAFARIS

THE BIG 5 AND MORE, WITHOUT (COMPLETELY) LOSING YOUR SHIRT

By Emily Janowsky

During our week on two different safaris through game reserves at opposite ends of Kruger National Park in South Africa, we had no problem seeing the Big 5 — lion, leopard, rhinoceros, elephant and Cape buffalo. In fact, on one of our drives, we came upon a herd of 75 elephants on the march. We tracked a pack of wild dogs, saw countless giraffe, hyenas, warthogs, and baboons, and marveled at a pod of hippos soaking in the river.

What amazed us most was the interactions between animals — something impossible to see in a zoo. Once, we came upon a female leopard who had dragged her kill into a tree. As she stared at the jeep, a large male leopard approached and stopped within two meters of our truck.

The two cats locked eyes and we held our breath. "I'm taking that," he telegraphed, and leaped into the tree, scooting the female onto a higher branch. As she tried in vain to make him leave, she lost her balance, fell from the tree, and ran off as the male took her lunch.

We exhaled. Wow.

We'd always wanted to take the kids to Africa, but like most travelers, we were afraid of the cost. Truth be told, there is no "cheap" way to fly halfway around the world, take a once-in-a-lifetime/bucket-list family vacation, and safely visit wild animals with your kids.

But I soon realized that the price of a family safari vacation descends from the stratosphere if you 1) book directly with a reputable safari outfitter, and 2) simply decrease the number of days you are on safari.

Most tourists want to make the most of the long flight and max out the length of their time in game parks — the most expensive portion of their African trip. But there are so many other interesting destinations in-country that don't require a guide and a truck and the expenses those entail.

Creating a varied itinerary in Africa worked perfectly for us. We began our 17-day vacation with a two-night layover in Dubai and then four nights in Cape Town, which helped us adjust to the time change and enabled us to see a completely different side of South Africa.

We split our final week between two game reserves near Kruger National Park — Kirkman's Kamp, in Sabi Sand on the southern end, and then Pafuri Camp, in Makuleke Reserve on the northern end where South Africa, Mozambique and Zimbabwe meet.

Kirkman's was everything I dreamed an African safari camp would be. Barney, our guide, and Eckson, our tracker, were amazing. The food, the setting, the service — it was all worth every pretty penny. Even though our expectations were high, they were exceeded. We loved, loved, loved it! ❖

THE GOOD STUFF

Kirkman's Kamp, Sabi Sand Private Reserve Kirkman's delivered a fantastic combination of accommodations and delicious food, layered with warm and gracious service. Our guide and tracker were amazing, so we had our best game drives here.

Pafuri Camp, Makuleke Reserve Set on a scenic riverside, this camp's tents were comfortable and gave off a classic safari feel. For birders or naturalists, this area would be especially perfect. We loved being able to view the animals from the decks of camp, but the game drives themselves were not as exciting as Kirkman's.

The ROAM Report

SOUTH AFRICA PRIVATE RESERVE SAFARIS

✚ Travelers: The Janowsky Family (parents plus two boys age 16 and 13)
✚ Date: June 2018
✚ Itinerary: A 17-day trip, including Dubai (2 nights), Cape Town (4 nights), and two South Africa game parks — Sabi Sand (3 nights) and Makuleke (3 nights)
✚ Cost: Approximately $30,000 for the entire vacation, including international and domestic flights, safaris, lodging, and tours
✚ Read more: bit.ly/roam2019safari

Îles de la Madeleine

LOVING CANADA'S HISTORIC ST. LAWRENCE BAY ARCHIPELAGO

By Claire Kerr-Zlobin

There, where the red sand from rocks washes into the ocean and deposits white sand on the beach, where the dunes rich in salt and islands have no trees, and where you feel completely at home and in an exotic, far-off land at the same time. Somewhere in the St. Lawrence Bay between Prince Edward Island (PEI) and Newfoundland lie the seven islands with a rich history that make up the Îles de la Madeleine islands. If you are looking for a Canadian destination that is completely off the beaten path, this is it.

Îles de la Madeleine is a magical paradise. Whether visiting as a family, a couple, or solo, there are endless things to see and do. Whether as an adventurer, nature lover, or just a person in need of downtime, you will find it all on Îles de la Madeleine. The accommodation levels range, and there is something for every type of traveler on every budget. Fair warning: you can't help but fall completely in love with Îles de la Madeleine — you'll want to return almost as soon as you leave.

SIX DAYS OF EXPLORING

After the 5-hour ferry from PEI, we arrived on Cap aux Meules, the unofficial gateway to the seven islands that make up Îles de la Madeleine. We explored the beach at our hotel, Chateau Madelinot, and walked its trails. Our kids loved the farm with so many animals to see.

On the hike at the Lighthouse on Île du Cap aux Meules, the contrast of the beautiful red sandbanks

and the piercing blue ocean captivated us. We started out at Cap Herisse and then headed over to Fatima and Cap-Vert. Their annual celebration is free to the public, and the clams and mussels taste divine! They had bouncy castles, sand boxes, music, and treats, so the kids loved it.

We explored three islands: Île du Havre-aux-Maisons, Grosse-Île, and Grand-Entrée. Leaving Havre-aux-Maisons, we stopped by the cheese factory, bakery, and smokehouse for grab and go lunch items. Midday we stopped at the local brewery (À l'abri de la Tempête) in L'Étang-du-Nord. We tried local food, including cheese and seal meat, and my hubby, Denys, sampled their locally produced beers. The beach, by the brewery, is lovely for exploring, and Denys spotted a shipwreck. Île du Havre-aux-Maisons is one of the islands with a treeless landscape — unusual in Canada and a bit shocking to see firsthand. Extensive logging in the 18th and 19th centuries deforested the island, rendering it treeless. That night, after checking into our Bubble tent accommodations at Auberge la Salicorne, we watched the sunset at the Grand-Entrée harbor.

Denys explored some of the amazing crawl/swim-through caves on the island, while the kids and I learned about the island and witnessed carnivorous plants up close. La Salicorne has English and French speaking guides. Our knowledgeable guide, Rosie, showed us carnivorous plants invisible to the naked eye through her magnifying glass.

Later we kayaked over to Île Boudreau, one of the small uninhabited islands, for yoga and a mud bath by the sea. The kids collected the special mud for our bath. After our mud dried, it was time for a cleansing dip in the ocean. In the evening, at low tide, we went clam digging and had so much fun! We dug up, cooked, and ate our dinner right on the beach. We spent our second night at La Salicorne in the inn, opting for the comforts of a traditional hotel room. A bonus — La Salicorne incorporates everything into their packages.

We earmarked a day for relaxation! It's awesome traveling with kids and the way to keep it so is to plan a relaxing day. So, that morning we went to Old Harry beach which, according to *National Geographic*, is one of the 10 most beautiful beaches in the world. The kids went to the kids' club and enjoyed crafts, games, and activities like pedal boats, kayaking, and stand up paddle boarding. They frolicked in the waves and sand with the staff, while we went off for a walk along the 8.5-kilometer beach. In the afternoon, Denys kayaked, and I opted for a massage. That evening we explored Ile de la Pointe aux Loups, a little township of 50 houses on the tiniest of the inhabited islands here.

The final day we explored a trail and beach on Havre aux Maisons and went on a fishing excursion to catch and then cook dinner back at our place in Parc du Gros Cap. ❖

The ROAM Report:

ÎLES DE LA MADELEINE, CANADA

+ **Travelers:** Claire, Denys and kids 10 and 5 when we visited.
+ **Date:** Summer 2017
+ **Itinerary:** Six nights in three locations: 2 nights at Hotel Chateau Mâdelinot, 2 nights in La Salicorne (one in a room and one in a camp) and 2 nights in the inn at Parc du Gros Cap
+ **Cost:** Rooms run under $150 per night
+ **Read more:** bit.ly/roam2019canada

The Good Stuff

Slow Pace

Away from the big city bustle, settle into a calmer pace. At times we felt like the only ones on the island. Whether it was hiking to the various lighthouses, walking on the pristine beaches, or enjoying the abundant watersports, there's lots to do. Book guided tours; most places have guides in both English and French.

Any Budget

This trip can be elaborate or simple. There are many accommodation and food options. Flights will be the biggest expense.

Winter Too

Winter delivers a completely different experience. We'd love to return to see the icefield and the harp seals. The sea is a bit choppy and can even be frozen, so flying in during winter is recommended.

By Liliia DeCos

TINIEST-EVER TREKKERS CONQUER NEPAL'S EPIC JOURNEY

If you're like us, you probably think that trekking to Everest Base Camp with kids is crazy. A year ago we thought the same thing, but we learned that the three-week trek is not as extreme or dangerous as many think. In fact, this trail is perfect for families with children, even young ones.

Our kids were 3 and 11 months old when they broke the unofficial world record and became the youngest-ever kids to set foot in Everest Base Camp on May 1, 2018. We were not aware of this until a guide told us the previous record holder was 4. While our "world record" status made us celebrities, it also made us question our sanity. We were confident, however, because we had done a ton of research and knew exactly how to do the trip in the safest way.

The entire journey was breathtaking. From dramatic vistas and high-altitude Tibetan Buddhist monasteries to the unique culture of Sherpas and other indigenous groups, the trek itself was incredible.

At times I couldn't trust my own eyes, the views were so epic. Our toddler's favorite word became "amazing" and our baby's first word was "wow."

Our biggest surprise was how much our kids loved it! Fresh air, friendly interactions, and all sorts of animals (yaks, horses, donkeys, pigs, goats, cats and dogs) were definite highlights. Not to mention, the trek was 24 days of their parents' full attention without phones, computers or distractions. Our relaxed pace allowed the kids to play while we drank tea at the Sherpa guesthouses. We enjoyed each other's company and bonded as a family.

The EBC trek is not as expensive as many believe, and not dangerous if you take simple precautions. Instead of rushing the hike, we would rest and refuel every few hours at a tea stall or guesthouse on the trail, making the trek far less challenging.

And in the future, who knows? Maybe one day we'll follow in our own footsteps in the Himalayas with our girls walking by our sides. ❖

The ROAM Report

EVEREST BASE CAMP TREK, NEPAL

Travelers: Liliia and Jose DeCos, plus 3-year-old and 11-month-old

Date: 24 days during April–May 2018

Itinerary: Kathmandu (2 nights) for sight-seeing and to gear up for the trek. Bus to Jiri (12 hours), hike to Everest Base Camp (18 days) return to Salleri (6 days), then bus back to Kathmandu (12 hours)

Cost: Approximately $1,300 for transport, lodging ($150), food ($800), and permits ($54 per adult)

Read more: bit.ly/roam2019nepal

EVEREST BASE CAMP TREK HIGHLIGHTS

Part 1: **From Jiri to Lukla**

Although many skip this section and fly directly to the new airport in Lukla, we loved this week of the trek. The scenery is great — you can even see Everest from one point — and the stretch allows you and your kids to acclimatize more slowly. It is on these less-traveled trails that you get to really experience the culture because there are fewer tourists. For example, we only saw 10 other trekkers during the days we traveled this section whereas after Lukla we saw 10 every five minutes.

Part 2: **Namche Bazaar**

At 3,200 meters, this town is the "base camp" to the Everest Base Camp trek and your last taste of luxury. We had our first yak steak here, and a salad with fresh vegetables. A salad might not sound exciting, but once you're past Namche it's a rarity. We stocked up on protein and chocolate bars, bought lots of yummy yak cheese, and got some locally woven socks and mittens for the little ones, just in case.

Part 3: **Namche to Base Camp**

This is the most challenging and rewarding part of the trek. The caravans passing by change from donkeys to yaks, the locals become noticeably indigenous, and the air thins into the freshest, cleanest air you've ever breathed. This part of the hike is worth taking slow as there is so much to enjoy.

I believe anyone can reach Everest Base Camp, some might just take a bit longer. We met an 80-year-old Israeli couple, a Canadian man without an arm and equipped with an artificial leg, a 4-month pregnant Finnish girl, and many others who are living proof that most of our perceived limits are only in our heads. If we made it, your family can too!

INTO THE HEART OF BORNEO

MISSES AND HITS IN THE DISAPPEARING RAINFORESTS OF INDONESIA

By Maryann Jones Thompson

After years of dreaming, months of buildup, two days on a plane, one day in a van, and 15 hours on a riverboat toward the heart of Borneo, my teen woke and said the words on everyone's minds.

"So where's the jungle?"

The clanking of our Indonesian *klotok*-turned-tourist-houseboat spurted to a halt along a floating dock in the village of Muara Muntai. The purply crack-of-dawn on the Mahakam River revealed nothing of the headhunter's headwaters I expected: No towering trees. No monkeys. No bustling Dayak longhouses.

But what our tech-addled family witnessed was equally otherworldly: A creek-clinging village buzzing to life. Fishermen revved moto-canoes to their nets. Girls in hijabs biked to school. A mom bathed her young son in the river.

Over our week on the main-

land in Indonesia's East Kalimantan state, we saw few tourists and unfortunately, only a few glimpses of the rapidly disappearing rainforests of "old" Borneo — hornbills, proboscis monkeys and Dayak totems.

We learned that to enjoy a trip to Borneo, you need to forget everything you think you know about the world's third largest island. You'll photograph epic riverfront villages (not rainforests), meet friendly locals (not headhunters), and be serenaded by tape recordings (not birds).

UP THE RIVER

We had landed two days prior in Balikpapan, the bustling capital of East Kalimantan and a pleasant, gleaming business center. Indonesia's Kalimantan states in Borneo are a bit like the American Midwest — a large expanse of natural resources to harvest. The rainforest is rapidly being cut down to plant palm oil plantations (largely due to U.S. policies) and gather the coal that lies near the surface.

Like all rivers in Borneo, the

The ROAM Report:

EAST KALIMANTAN, BORNEO, INDONESIA

+ **Travelers:** Maryann & Don Thompson and their kids aged 15 and 17
+ **Date:** 1 week in August 2018, as part of a 3-week trip in Indonesia
+ **Cost:** $2,250 for all transport, meals, guides and entrance fees for four people for five days with Borneo De 'Gigant Tours
+ **Read more:** bit.ly/roam2019borneo

storied and mighty Mahakam is the lifeblood and main transportation artery for the area, moving people and goods to tiny and huge towns throughout the state. The river that used to carry intrepid explorers, traders, and more recently, tourists, into the heart of Borneo to study the rainforest and Dayak life now serves as a highway for unbelievably giant barges loaded down with logs or coal heading to the port in Balik-papan.

These barges and an almost unbroken line of towns were all we saw during our first afternoon on the houseboat. "Just wait!" I had said to Pearl. "Tomorrow morning we will wake up in the jungle."

Our houseboat home for four days was tricked out for tourists — spotlessly clean with a friendly crew and darling grandma cook. Our eating and sleeping quarters were huge — the whole boat was huge — and we felt like a rajah's entourage until we saw an older German couple the next day who actually had booked the "rajah" houseboat: Their deck hands had

uniforms and their chairs were not made of plastic.

Wandering Muara Muntai and other Mahakam villages, we encountered motorcycles, bikes and other townspeople moving around on raised boardwalks. We realized that the entire town was built to float during high waters of the wet season. The river was truly the heart of the town, with locals coming to the dock for all of their needs.

"Hear the birds? So amazing!" I said, trying to psych up everyone — including myself — and get the kids to forget it was their third day of the trip without wifi and jungle.

"Oh no, those are not birds," said our guide. "Those are tape recordings." Indeed, the entire Mahakam basin was filled with the sound of chirping swallows, a recording that was broadcast 24 hours a day from the top of huge windowless buildings that look like the Jawa Sandcrawler transports on Tatooine in *Star Wars*. The locals build these barn-type structures in hopes of attracting swallows to live there and return every year; they harvest their nests to sell to the Chinese for soup. We then remembered our friend Kris had shown us similar structures in southern Cambodia. Soon, I'm sure, the call of swallows will reverberate throughout rural Southeast Asia.

LONGHOUSE GHOST TOWN

We headed out for the day in a moto-canoe. Instead of a rainforest, we traversed a massive marsh, Jempang Lake, with grasses and egrets as we see near home in San Francisco. The lack of trees was made up for by scenes of fishermen up to their necks in water, placing poles, hanging nets, and shoving a hand in the air to wave "hello" as we passed. After a couple hours, we reached Mancong village, where a group of high school kids in a cafe got up the courage to chat with our kids.

Our destination was the Tanjung Isuy Dayak longhouse, one of the oldest and most impressive in Borneo. These massive buildings are surrounded by hundreds of carved figures and served as the centers of village life. And though today's tourism folks downplay the "headhunter" talk, our guide told us that the skulls of enemy tribes used to hang from the rafters. Families cooked and lived in apartment-type rooms along the main floor and kept livestock underneath.

But in August 2018, this longhouse was a ghost town. We had been worried about having to watch a fake tribal dance but we actually saw no one. The longhouse is a preserved national monument now, and we knew that no one has lived inside for a long time. But there were no other tourists there and no one running the place. We walked through the adjacent village in the sweltering heat and saw where the original villagers now live, but in the midday heat, there wasn't much life going on at all. And my natives were restless — or listless — or both.

ORANGUTANS IN THE WILD

We knew taking our teens to Borneo required some careful planning. Most tourists do one of three things: Visit Sabah in the Malaysian north, houseboat through the heavily touristed orangutan conservation area of Tanjung Puting National Park in the Indonesian south, or head to East Kalimantan, where visitors can see wild orangutans in Kutai National Park. That chance, together with the Mahakam houseboat and the Derawan Islands for scuba diving pushed us to go east.

But I never did a good job, pre-trip, reconciling the virgin-rainforested Borneo I'd read about in the 1980s classic *Into the Heart of Borneo* with the reality of Borneo today. The poor Kutai National Park and its orangutans are waiting to be bulldozed. Sleeping overnight in the horribly rundown park guesthouse, you can hear chainsaws and earthmovers at work. A devastating forest fire consumed the area in 2015 and the government used it as an opportunity to seize the coal and lumber and shrink the park boundaries.

We hiked two different days through old-growth rainforest and saw a host of fantastic jungle creatures, including the biggest tarantula we've ever seen. And we were lucky to see many orangutans. We got to see mamas with babies. We got to see big guys galumph from treetop to treetop, dropping an avalanche of leaves and branches along the way. But their territory is so small now that it's only a matter of time before their time is up in Kutai.

THE REAL CHALLENGE

Back on the houseboat, we had headed up a different, smaller creek through even smaller villages and finally escaped civilization. There we saw the Borneo of legend: troops of macaques and proboscis monkeys in the trees, hornbills flying overhead, and big monitor lizards on the riverbank. But our time there felt fleeting — and after a half day, we returned to the houseboat and the buzzing villages.

But the real disappointment we faced in Borneo was the "getting sick." Not just sick, but "India sick." I was so worried about the kids getting eaten by mosquitos that I took my eye off the ball: The river. So when Don suddenly went running for the bathroom and spent the next 12 hours curled in the fetal position in various locations around the houseboat, I became a nervous wreck: We were all on the same boat eating the same food and drinking the same water. Nevermind that the galley was so clean I would have eaten off the floor, Don got sick. And that meant we would all be sick, too. Any minute.

But as travel mysteries happen, no one else got sick. And Don rejoined the land of the living the very next morning. But my traveling-mom poker face was gone. I had shown my hand to the kids and they realized I was on edge. "Don't eat that shrimp." "Wipe the water off the edge of that dish." "No more fruit." Then, as if on cue, the houseboat's generator quit working, which meant

no fan at night. So sleeping quit happening, too. Morale sank accordingly.

A DIFFERENT ADVENTURE

Looking back on the challenges of the journey, I'd do it again in a second. Places like the villages of the Mahakam River may as well be on the moon, they are so fascinating and foreign. And the houseboat tours make it easy to see what used to require an expedition. The truth is, anyone like me who has long dreamed of seeing Borneo's people, wildlife and forests has no choice but to go now and see what's left — before it, too, is gone.

Back in Balikpapan, a shower felt great after a week of rivers, roads, and rainforest. Wifi warmed my teens' hands and hearts. The handful of Dutch, Belgian and French tourists we met at the hotel were as intrigued and excited about East Kalimantan as we were. They'd had different highs and lows but vowed to come back, too.

Traveling in Borneo is still a truly amazing adventure — even if it's not the adventure we came for. ❖

EXPLORING THE WHITE MOUNTAINS

By Valentine J. Brkich

Each August before school begins, my wife, kids, and I pack ourselves (and way too much stuff) into our Hyundai and head 12 hours north to the scenic White Mountains of New Hampshire. Mountains in New Hampshire, you ask? Yep. Big, beautiful ones too — the kind that reach into the clouds and seem to call out to you to come and explore their secret, lofty heights.

We stay in Lincoln, known for its challenging ski slopes, quaint main drag, and proximity to some of the area's most stunning natural wonders. Lincoln has everything from Airbnbs to four-star resorts, and whether we're in the mood to hike a mountain, swim in an icy-cold stream, or maybe do a little shopping, this area has it all.

Lincoln is situated along the Kancamagus Scenic Byway (Rt. 112), aka "The Kanc"— a 34.5-mile, winding, two-lane highway that snakes its way through the 800,000-acre White Mountain National Forest. Known for its scenic vistas and stunning fall foliage, it's one of the most peaceful, memorable drives you'll ever take.

In neighboring North Woodstock, we discovered Cascade Park and found a picture-postcard scene of white water rushing over immense boulders and slabs of granite, bordered on both sides by lush mountain greenery. This small section of the Pemigewasset River was the perfect place to cool off in the late-summer heat. You can even rent inflatable tubes in town for $5 and brave the rapids, if you have the courage. (I did not.)

So what can one do whilst visiting the White Mountains? Besides a whole lotta nothing (which, personally, is what I like to do), there are innumerable outdoor activities and adventures to choose from. Make a point to visit this little slice of heaven in upper New England — and don't miss our family's faves. ❖

Top 5 Countdown:
White Mountains

#5 Take a Hike

With over 1,200 miles of scenic, well-maintained trails, the White Mountains are a hiking enthusiast's dream. From lazy day hikes to uber-challenging multi-day jaunts, there's a trail for just about every level of hiker up in them thar hills.

This year we hiked up Mt. Willard. This moderate, 3.2-mile round-trip hike follows an old carriage trail up most of the mountain and makes for a great family-friendly adventure. The trailhead starts at the Crawford Notch Railroad Station, and winds its way to the 2,815 foot summit. Along the way, you can stop for a photo or cool off in Centennial Falls just off the trail. When you emerge from the trail at the top of the mountain, the effect is breathtaking. Although I enjoyed the view, I spent most of my time herding my thrill-seeking wife and kids away from the edge of the cliff.

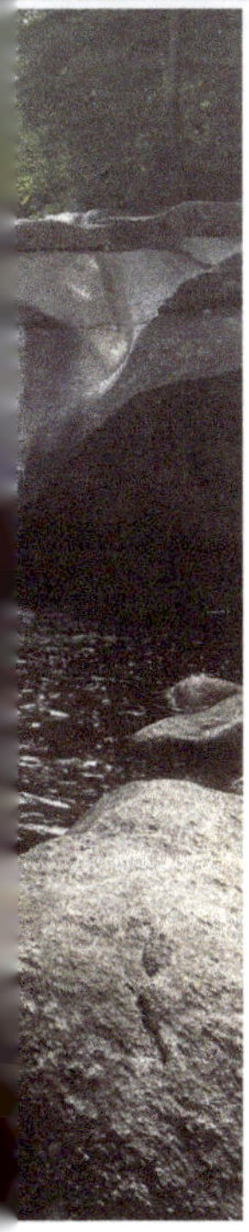

#4 Make a Splash

One thing we wanted to do for sure this year was find a secluded spot where we might dip our toes (and possibly more) in the icy yet invigorating mountain waters.

We loved Diana's Baths near Bartlett. After a super-easy 0.6-mile hike along a wide, packed-gravel path, we arrived at the "baths," a series of huge rocks, ledges, pools, and cascading falls smack dab in the middle of the woods. The kids took off immediately to climb amongst the rocks and splash in the frigid yet oh-so-refreshing streams.

#1 Lost River Gorge & Boulder Caves

On our first trip to New Hampshire, some good friends who regularly visit thev Granite State recommended we check out the Lost River Gorge & Boulder Caves. This natural wonder has since become one of our favorite parts of our annual visit.

Lost River Gorge & Boulder Caves gives visitors the chance to explore more than 20 caves and natural formations in Kinsman Notch, a breathtaking wonder of rock and boulder formations formed over eons by water, wind, and weather. Visitors descend 300 feet down into the gorge before following a 1-mile boardwalk (an engineering wonder in itself) through a labyrinth of massive granite boulders and stunning waterfalls back to the top.

Lost River's caves are a blast to crawl through as you gradually make your way back to the top of the gorge. Each one has a different name — Cave of Silence, Bear Crawl, Shadow Cave — and each offers a new and exciting challenge. Many of the caves require you to crawl on your hands and knees (or even your belly) through the darkness as you make your way toward the light of the exit. The only cave I couldn't conquer was the infamous Lemon Squeezer. (I wasn't flexible enough to make it through the opening! Not surprising considering I can't touch my toes.) But if you're the claustrophobic type, don't worry: A boardwalk allows you to bypass all the caves while still taking in all the subterranean formations.

#3 Moose Spotting

Yes, there are moose in New Hampshire — approximately, 3,000–4,000 at last count. There are moose-crossing signs all along The Kanc and surrounding highways warning drivers to be on the lookout for these enormous creatures. (A full-grown adult can reach 6-feet high at the shoulder and weigh in excess of 1,000 pounds!)

I've yet to come across one of these majestic beasts during my time in the White Mountains. My eyes have been peeled, but alas, I haven't been in the right spot at the right time. Nearly every evening my wife's cousin takes us moose hunting (albeit with a camera rather than a rifle) along The Kanc, hitting up his "secret spots" where he's always sure we'll come across one of these elusive beasts of the North. The only moose we've ever encountered? A fake one on the way up Mt. Washington.

#2 Ride the Cog

In Pittsburgh, we have the Monongahela Incline and the Duquesne Incline — two funicular railways that take riders up and down the city's Mt. Washington (or as we Yinzers call it, *Mt. Warsh-ington*). At 1,200 feet, the summit gives visitors a stunning view of downtown and the three rivers below.

In New Hampshire they have a Mt. Washington, too, only it's 6,288 feet high. And instead of an incline, they have the Mount Washington Cog Railway, aka "The Cog."

The Cog is the world's first mountain-climbing cog railway. Each day two steam locomotives and six biodiesel-powered locomotives carry thrill-seekers to the top of the mountain along a narrow, 3-mile track that straddles heart-stopping, 1,000-foot-plus ledges and at times reaches a maximum grade of 37.41 percent. Luckily it moves at a leisurely, tortoise-like pace of 2.8 mph and gives riders a little over an hour to take in the stunning views of the Presidential Range and beyond.

VISIT OFFSEASON FOR ALL THE ACTION AND MORE "OLD" CALIFORNIA

Everyone but the dogs and cats came to Catalina: The kids, aunts, uncles, cousins, grandparents, and parents docked in the picturesque Avalon, just an hour's ferry from the Southern California coast.

We aimed to ring in the 2019 New Year together, but our paths to that midnight were divergent. Everyone had a list of must-dos: We were looking forward to two days of scuba diving; my brother's family planned a big hike; my sister's toddlers wanted to ride the submarine; Grandpa and Grammy planned a happy-hour tour; and every kid was psyched for ziplining and mini golf.

Catalina is an ideal destinations for multigenerational trips. All members of any family can spend their days running in opposite directions, doing exactly as they please, and still meet up for a game of pre-dinner tag in the sand, a golf cart trip up the hill, or a trip to the candy store.

What surprised us all about Catalina was its authentic Old California vibe. Just as most Yellowstone tourists never move 500 feet from a road, most Catalina visitors never move 500 feet from Crescent Avenue, the seaside promenade lined with happy restaurants and bars. And though the boardwalk is a lively place for a stroll, it's only the beginning of what the island has to offer.

Our off-season week showed us the depth of the island's true character: Not only do its natural landscapes show visitors what the state looked like pre-development, but Avalon is a living and breathing example of a West Coast tourist town frozen in time.

The ROAM Report

CATALINA ISLAND, CALIFORNIA

+ Travelers: Multigenerational trip, with three sets of parents, one set of grandparents, and six cousins

+ Date: Five nights around New Year's Day 2019

+ Cost: Winter cottage rental ran about $500 per night for six people. Return ferry from Long Beach costs approximately $75 per person.

+ Read more: bit.ly/roam2019catalina

Hikers can trek for days across the island through hills covered in oak, cactus and chaparral, and be rewarded with stunning vistas of the Pacific.

The island boasts the longest undeveloped coastline in the state, and 60 plant and animal species found nowhere else on Earth. The island's famous bison herd once numbered near 600 but is now managed at around 180.

In the end, Catalina delivered far more than a seaside getaway for our extended family. Yes, there were nonstop things-to-do and yes, we loved the whole place — from the people to the town, the reef to the hills. But we also got a glimpse of our fabulous Southern Californian ancestry — the mission, rancho, seafaring, silver screen, artisan, beach-going, nature-loving ethos that made this state into the mecca it is today. ❖

THE GOOD STUFF

Scuba Diving with Kids on Catalina

The island is one of the most popular places for scuba diving in all of California and a great place for families to do their first open water dives. Catalina Divers Supply guides and captains deliver professional, safe and fun days on the water for both experienced and novice divers.

Water Activities for Non-Divers

There are plenty of options for getting out on Catalina's water without breathing compressed air. The Catalina Island Company is the epicenter for all island activities, including boat excursions, snorkel/scuba trips, and more. And right in Avalon Harbor, glass bottom boats and submarines let non-divers see big schools of fish and kelp. (The submarine is not for the claustrophobic or those prone to motion sickness, however.)

Hiking Around the Airport in the Sky

For day trips into the island's interior, book the Conservancy's Wildland Express shuttle to Two Harbors or to Airport in the Sky. Head across the top of the hills for gorgeous vistas and keep an eye out for buffalo, deer, squirrels and foxes — the only mammals living on the island's land.

The most little-kid-friendly trail is the flat Airport Loop, which meanders around the runway for an hour and provides views of the native flora.

The Conservancy web site details every hike on the island, including half-day, full-day and multi-day treks. All hikers need a permit that is obtainable online for same-day treks.

Movies & Tours at the Catalina Casino

Originally designed as a dance hall, Art Deco Catalina Casino is widely recognized as the island's landmark building. Casino tours run daily and are a must for historical and architectural buffs.

Families will love the nightly first-run films that screen in the sumptuous ground floor movie theater — the first in the world built to screen "talkies."

Family Bike Rentals on Catalina

Bike rentals are widely available on the island — in fact, many hotels include them for guests.

Mountain biking is serious business on Catalina. Trails cross the entire interior and multi-day trips are possible for avid bikers and their kids.

Cruise a Golf Cart

No kid will visit Catalina without wanting to rent a golf cart. The whining will begin upon arrival and continue until a seat belt clicks across their lap. Riding up and down Avalon's downtown streets and up into the hills above the town is a blast for the whole family.

Beach Time and Ziplines at the Descanso Beach Club

The weird thing about Catalina is that for an island, it really isn't all about swimming and sunning (especially in late December) but maybe that's the reason why there are so many other things to do! There are few swimming pools and the main beach in Avalon is tiny. If you're wanting a chaise and some sand in your toes, head to Catalina Island Company's Descanso Beach Club, where you'll find a long rocky beach, restaurant, and trails. Descanso is also the base for the Aerial Adventure ropes course, Climbing Wall, and the eagerly anticipated Zip Line Eco Adventure! It isn't cheap, but if you can only do one land-based activity on the island, this is it. Five runs descend 600 feet of elevation back down to the beach, with epic vistas the entire way.

FAMILY GALAPAGOS
on a Budget

By Nicola "Poz" Poswillo

SEE EARTH'S NATURAL SPECTACLE FOR LESS

Tortoises, sea lions, rays, iguanas, flamingos, penguins — and boobies! Hiking, snorkeling, boating and biking — the Galapagos has so much to see and do. The islands had been on my brood's bucket list for a really long time but could we really do it together, while the kids still wanted to be with us and while we were still spry enough to roam without a walker? And what about the expense? I wasn't sure it was doable as a family vacation considering we were coming from our home in New Zealand with 9-year-old twin daughters and a 12-year-old son in tow.

So we started saving — a lot.

It was a lengthy process to decide when to go and how to see the Galapagos on a budget as there are many, many options to consider. First, you need to fly to the islands from Ecuador — no

where else. Then, there are land- and water-based trips; 4-, 8- and 8-plus day options; economy, "superior," first-class and luxury boats; motorboats and yachts; boats with 12–100 people. Bewildering.

After reading all about it, we decided to save a bit harder and do an 8-day motorboat trip on the Eden. Though it sounds splurge-y, it actually is the best use of a family's Galapagos budget and time. Here's why:

■ Day 1 is arrival and Day 8 is departure, so that essentially gave us 6 full days of exploring.

■ A boat trip, while more expensive, ensured we had maximum time exploring the Galapagos sites and minimized the daily travel to and from land-based hotels.

■ If the children wanted to sleep in, they wouldn't miss early departure times.

■ It's costly to get to and from the Galapagos (approximately a 90-minute flight from mainland Ecuador); this doesn't change with length of boat trip.

■ It's a $100 national park fee per person ($50 for children under 12) no matter how many days you stay.

■ Yachts don't move as fast as motorboats, so they generally don't go to the outer islands.

■ Even though our boat itinerary only explored the eastern half of the Galapagos, we easily added on a few days at the end of our tour to independently travel to Isla Isabella, the largest island in the Galapagos, where there are daily boats and plentiful hostels.

When I booked directly with the boat, they ended up offering me the "last-minute" prices three months prior to departure, with a discount for the kids under 12. This was the best option for us, as securing our Galapagos beds meant we could then book flights through the airlines (and not pay last-minute expensive fares) and then make plans for the rest of our trip.

Choosing an off-peak time of year also helped us get the cruise for less. The Galapagos has peak and nonpeak times of the year and months when the water is warmer. We decided on May, outside of Christmas and Easter holidays; outside of July and August when much of the world is on holiday; and at a time of the year when the water isn't too chilly, enabling us more time to explore the marine life of the Galapagos. It was also the month with OK weather in the part of the mainland where we would spend the rest of our trip.

Overall, the Galapagos lived up to the hype for our family — it was a real adventure, with some huge learning for the children. It was expensive but well worth it — and it was all paid for a few months before we left, so we didn't come home to a huge bill! ❖

The ROAM Report

GALAPAGOS

+ **Travelers:** Poz (Mum), Steve (Dad), and kids 12, 9, and 9 years
+ **Date:** May 2017
+ **Itinerary:** Two weeks—8 days by boat with a land-based add-on of Isla Isabella — in the eastern Galapagos.
+ **Cost:** Galapagos 8-day, all-expenses-paid tour: $11,500; national park fees: $400 on arrival; roundtrip flights from Quito to Galapagos: $1,500); interisland water taxis: $30 per person
+ **Read more:** bit.ly/roam2019/galapagos

LOVING LISBON, LAGOS & BEYOND

WHY PORTUGAL IS EUROPE'S HOTTEST FAMILY DESTINATION

By Dina Harrison

Imagine waking up to see a fort — outside your window!?! We rouse the kids and head out, following our noses and our iPhones in search of coffee and pastries. The vibrant street art, lively waterfront and serious hills underfoot remind us of home in San Francisco — there's even a red suspension bridge spanning the Tagus River to match the Golden Gate! But the bright azulejo-tiled buildings, delicious aromas and historic alleys tell us we're somewhere completely different.

This is Lisbon. And these steps were just the beginning of neighborhood-after-neighborhood, town-after-town delights for ourselves and our kids during our summer stay in Portugal.

The kids were drawn to Portugal by the idea of seeing the westernmost and southernmost point in all of Europe. My husband and I came for the other reasons so many families spend their summers in this corner of Iberia: the ideal weather, epic landscape, architecture, history, food and culture all layered atop Portugal's reputation for being

one of the safest and most affordable countries in Europe.

In the end, our kids seemed to find adventure around every corner. Whether it was walking along the city walls, climbing the steps to a castle, or counting the steps to our apartment, it was always an adventure!

Our kids begged us to start our Lisbon explorations at the fort we could see from our window, the Castelo São Jorge. It's on top of the hill overlooking both the Atlantic Ocean and the city of Lisbon. It's a

bit of a climb to the top but once you are there, the views are fantastic! The kids loved playing on the cannons and walking along the walls of the fort.

From there, we meandered down into the Alfama neighborhood, checking out the tiny roads, souvenir shops and cobblestone streets. We hopped on a tuk-tuk-type vehicle and the driver took us around for a little bit. We headed to the Baixa neighborhood next. We were on a mission to check out A Cevicheria. The food and ceviche

were wonderful and we all loved the octopus sculpture hanging from the ceiling!

Belém was our next neighborhood to explore. It's easy to take the train there and back from the main station in Lisbon, and the main attraction is the seaside Tower of Belém. The area is also home to pastel de nata egg custard tarts, and the ones found at the original mothership, Pastéis de Belém, are, no joke, delicious. They're definitely worth waiting for and the line moves quickly. We then toured the Jerónimos Monastery and Church while we let the heavenly pastries digest and then saw the famous Monument of the Discoveries, which honors the many Portuguese explorers.

A day trip to Sintra is a must-do and will take a whole day. It is easiest to take a train there as parking is very limited. It's a bit of a racket when you get off the train because there is a bus that does a loop so you then pay for the bus to take you up the hill. It's too long a walk, though, because you'd lose precious time at the museums and castles. We did the train then bus and it was fine.

We hit the amazing Castle of the Moors, then the famous Pena Palace then had lunch in town. After that, we saw some of the lesser known houses and castles and loved that we had more space in which to see them as the crowds had moved to the places we had already seen. The UNESCO World Heritage castle is the most breathtaking — the colors on the exterior alone are Instagram-worthy!

Another day-trip-worthy place is Estoril. It's a pretty beach town with a boardwalk where people stroll in the afternoons. It's quite the scene, especially on weekends. It also lets you see a wealthier suburb just outside of Lisbon.

ON TO THE ALGARVE

After our days exploring Lisbon, we rented a car and headed south toward the Algarve region. After about three hours, we hit the Lighthouse of Cabo de São Vicente, which is the farthest southwest point in all of Portugal — and Europe. By luck, the light-house keeper was there and gave us and another family a tour of the lighthouse. It was really cool and something we didn't expect

After playing on the steep cliffs (and scaring this mommy), we jumped back in the car for one more hour to Lagos. Lagos is the more mellow of the towns of the Algarve region.

We stayed in an apartment near Praia Dona Ana beach which was one of the best beaches in all of Portugal. We loved the rocks and the "tunnels" you could swim through during low and high tide.

During our time at the beach, we spent many hours just relaxing on the beach, making sand castles, collecting shells, swimming and hunting for crabs. One day, we rented kayaks and a guide led us into many coves and tunnels. We loved seeing all these wonderful secret spots that are not accessible by land.

And what could end our stay better than watching Portugal's soccer team win the EuroCup. The whole town of Lagos went crazy — and celebrated into the early morning hours. Such an awesome time to be in Portugal! ❖

The ROAM Report

PORTUGAL

✦ **Travelers:** Dina and Steve Harrison and their kids, 9 and 7 years old
✦ **Date:** July 2016
✦ **Itinerary:** 4 days in Lisbon and 5 days in the Algarve
✦ **Cost:** About $200 a night for lodging and another $100 for activities, food and transport — very reasonable for Europe!
✦ **Read more:** bit.ly/roam2019portugal

Three Tips for Portugal

1

Walking Shoes
Lisbon is a walking city and it's very hilly. Be prepared with good walking shoes.

2

Phones Matter
Cell service is super helpful for Google Maps, the train and bus schedules, dinner reservations and even museum tickets.

3

Airbnb Questions
Ask the owner about the unit's location: Is it on top of a hill? How many steps to the door? This info is critical when traveling with grandparents or young kids.

PARADISE IN THE PHILIPPINES

CORON, PALAWAN AND MORE BUDGET ISLAND HOPS

By Liliia DeCos

When travelers want "Southeast Asia," most aim for Thailand, Vietnam, and Bali. For some reason, the Philippines remain an under-the-radar destination. But after six months of traveling throughout the region, we believe the opposite should be true: If you only have time for one country, go to the Philippines. And if you only have time for one area, make it the islands of Coron and Palawan.

Palawan has featured prominently in the "world's best beaches"-type lists in the last decade or so, especially since another Philippine paradise — Boracay — became so overtouristed that it was shut down by the government and reopened with new restrictions on visitors. As tourists to the Palawan area increase, we can only hope the country will not make the same mistake twice.

The good news is that Palawan is quite large and its stunning neighbor, Coron, is a national park with few overnight accommodations. These tropical islands are quite simply a paradise on Earth: pristine water, remote islets, hidden bays, coral reefs, and WWII shipwrecks.

You can spend the whole time relaxing or being active — there's snorkeling, diving, canoeing, kayaking, and hiking — or some combo of both. And where else in the world can you boat to day after day of new reefs, paddle an underground river, and camp on a deserted island?

If you've only got a week or two, the Philippines can be more expensive than neighboring countries because flying from island to island can definitely eat up a budget. But for families who have more time, taking boats, buses and staying in smaller places, the country is as affordable as other Southeast Asian countries.

We found many compelling spots while hopping across a handful of the country's 7,641 islands, but without a doubt the most beautiful part of the Philippines is its people. The locals give off a very kind, helpful and cheerful vibe. Their English is excellent so it isn't difficult to communicate. And Filipinos love children and love to show it: Traveling with our blonde daughter made us the main attraction with the locals, regardless of what attraction we were visiting.

After traveling around the world with our kids for several years, the Philippines remains one of our favorite countries and we can't wait to return. With so much to see and do, we've got at least 7,630 islands to go. ❖

THE PHILIPPINES

Travelers: Liliia & Jose DeCos, plus their baby daughter

Date: February 2016

Itinerary: Manila (3 nights), Coron (5 nights), El Nido (Palawan, 3 nights), and Puerto Princesa (Palawan, 3 nights), Manila (1 night), Legazpi (1 night), Donsol (3 nights), Tagbilaran (Bohol Island, 4 nights)

Cost: Approximately $45–$65 per day, including $15 to $25 per night for accommodations, $10–$20 per day for food and transport, and $20 per day for activities (excluding diving)

Read more: bit.ly/roam2019philippines

THE GOOD STUFF

Reefs of Coron Island

We took a boat from Manila to Coron Town and stayed there for five nights. The famous Coron Island is part of a national park so we stayed in Coron Town and did a different boat trip every day. We were swimming, lazing, floating and snorkeling all day, every day in one of the most beautiful places in the world! The crew members cooked fresh fish, vegetables and rice for lunch right on the spot in front of us — it couldn't have been fresher! Scuba divers should not miss Coron's WWII Japanese shipwrecks.

Deserted Island near El Nido

El Nido is a small town on Palawan Island with the same type of activities as Coron Town but for twice the price and with three times as many people, because the island has an airport. But one of the most unique and memorable adventures in our traveling life — by far — happened near El Nido: Camping on an uninhabited island in the South China Sea. We rented gear and a boat and slept on the beach. We made a small bonfire, cooked dinner over the coals, played guitar and sang songs until late — unforgettable!

Underground River in Puerto Princesa

We went to Puerto Princesa specifically for another otherworldly experience: Paddling down an underground river. When we read about boating through tiny, narrow, underground caves in a little boat where only a boatman's lamp guides the way, we knew we had to do it. Everyone receives an audio guide, so the whole tour happens in complete silence. They do it this way so as not to disturb the cave's ecosystem. For the visitor, it is equally satisfying — especially if you remove your headphones along the way and simply listen to the bats and the "silence" in the cave.

Mayon Volcano near Legazpi

The Mayon volcano is the most active volcano in the Philippines — it last erupted in 2018! But that's not why it draws tourists from everywhere in the world: Mayon has a perfectly symmetric conical shape and it is known as a "perfect cone" volcano. The mountain delivers a true postcard view! There is a nice kid-friendly volcano park and viewpoint nearby.

Whale Sharks in Donsol

We ticked another item off our bucket list in the Philippines: Swimming with the whale sharks. Donsol is the only eco-friendly way to see and interact with these gentle giants. Their eco-tourism conservation program is set up and monitored by the WWF. While you cannot be guaranteed of seeing the world's biggest fish, we got lucky! Every minute we spent in the water with these whale sharks was a gift.

Chocolate Hills and Tarsiers on Bohol Island

There are two reasons to visit Bohol Island: See the unique, mound-dotted landscape of the Chocolate Hills and meet the world's smallest primate at the Tarsier Conservation Center — you can even do both in one day by renting a motorbike or taking a tour.

Taal Volcano near Manila

You can see all the sights of Manila — churches, forts, parks, seaside — in a day or two. The real reason you need to visit is to trek to the smallest active volcano in the world, Taal. It is truly spectacular because it's not just a simple volcano — it is on an island in a lake, and on that island, there is another lake with an island topped by the volcano. Wow! Kids love the trip because it involves a bit of hiking or horseback riding to get up the mountain.

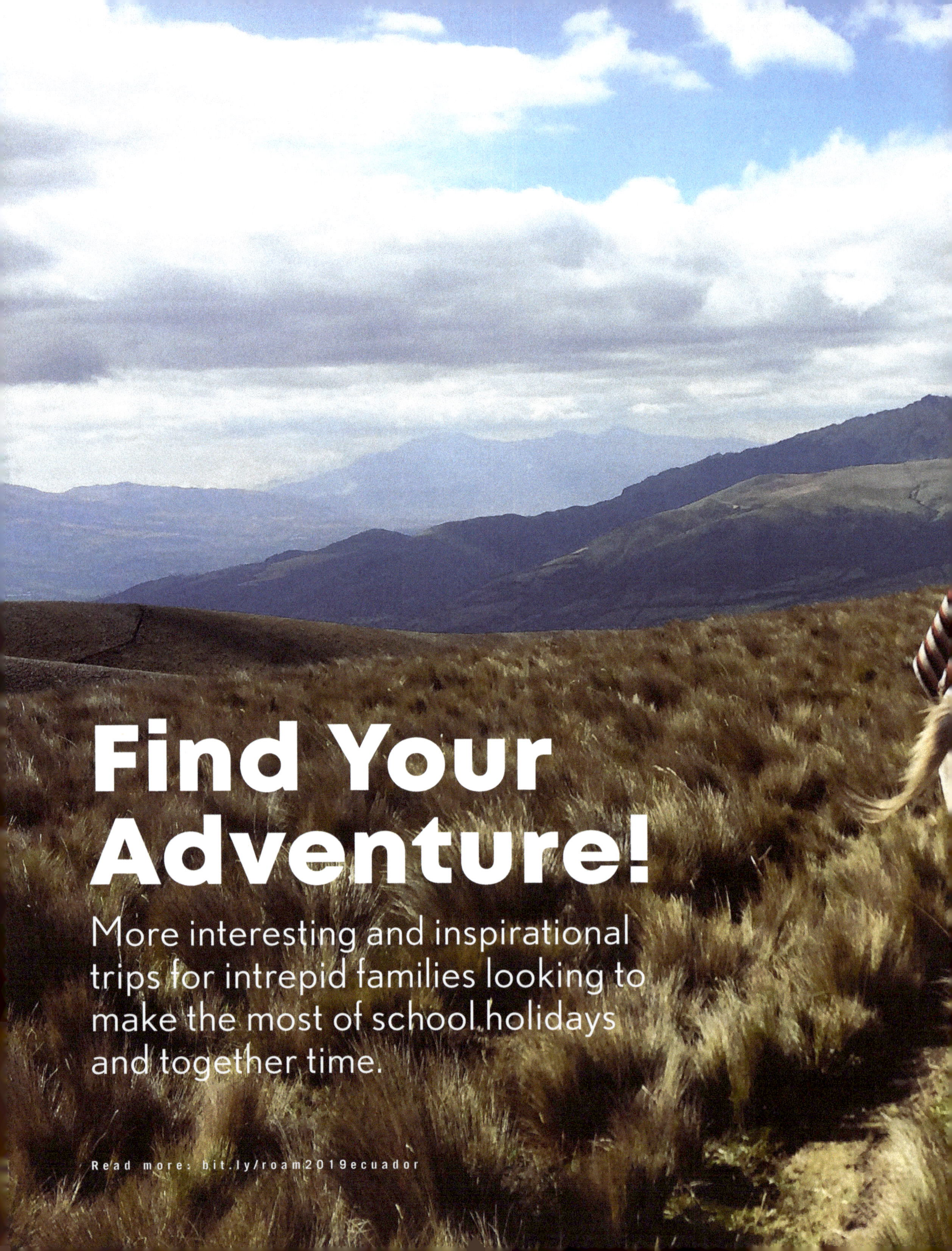

Find Your Adventure!

More interesting and inspirational trips for intrepid families looking to make the most of school holidays and together time.

Read more: bit.ly/roam2019ecuador

Winter Wilds of Yellowstone

An epic expedition of snow, steam & solitude

It was -28°F — but it was a dry -28°. There were no clouds, no wind, and no crowds. After a morning of other-worldly views on the snowcoach ride to Yellowstone's Snow Lodge, we watched Old Faithful erupt with just a few dozen folks before heading out across the Upper Geyser basin on one of the most extraordinary day hikes of our lives: We passed bison grazing in the snow, geysers belching steam, ponds bubbling with various, multi-colored liquids, and trees coated with clumps of geothermally enhanced snow.

We had driven 1,200 miles in two days, from Christmas in sunny Southern California to New Year's in icy northern Yellowstone. We entered the world's first national park near Bozeman, Montana and stayed at Mammoth Hot Springs so that we could drive through the Lamar Valley–the only road open to private vehicles in the winter. On the half-day drive, we saw few cars but many elk, bighorn sheep, otter, moose, and bison eking out their January existence atop yards of powder.

Yes, it was freezing. Yes, we all endured a bout of flu-like illness. Yes, my son did the whole snowy week on crutches. And yes, we would do it again in a heartbeat. Hands down, Yellowstone is the best winter road trip in America, a must-see spectacle that is worth every dollar, minute, and shiver you can muster. — *Don Thompson*

Read more: bit.ly/roam2019yellowstone

Winter in Denali
Snowshoe, ski, and drive in Alaska's backcountry

Residents of the Last Frontier would like to make one thing perfectly clear: "Alaska is not closed in the winter." Most curious would-be winter visitors harbor the belief that Alaska's popular summertime destinations like Denali National Park shut their front gates once Labor Day weekend passes.

Denali and the small communities around this 9,492-square-mile national park are wide open during the non-summer months, welcoming adventurous families with a plethora of recreation options, as long as said families are prepared for the large, yet interesting differences between summer and winter. — *Erin Kirkland*

Read more: bit.ly/roam2019alaska

Christmas in Chamonix
A season of sparkle, not snowpack

It is almost indescribable how beautiful Chamonix is in wintertime. The tiny French hamlet sits in a valley nestled between Mt. Blanc and the tips of a dozen other Alpine peaks. The lifts whisk skiers from the village to the top of the mountain. The village twinkles with Christmas everywhere. The locals are lovely and welcoming.

After years of planning, our Christmas in Chamonix was really happening! And it was picture perfect–except for one thing: The snow. There wasn't enough to ski! But our Alpine Noel proved unforgettable, with gooey Christmas fondue, epic views, skiing in Italy and–who'd have guessed?–paragliding in the Alps! — *Belinda O'Neil*

Read more: bit.ly/roam2019chamonix

Colorado for Non-Skiers
Irresistible Rocky Mountain thrills

Colorado is renowned as a downhill skier's paradise, but it's plenty of snow-covered fun for nonskiers, too. From ice climbing to skijoring to snowkiting — yes, you read that right — there are many family-friendly wintertime activities even non-skiers can enjoy throughout the Centennial State.

One of our favorites is the dog-sledding program at YMCA's Snow Mountain Ranch (SMR) in Granby. The property offers the usual array of winter activities: ice skating, tubing, fat-biking, Nordic-skiing and more. But the most popular attraction is the dog sledding, looping two miles through the open meadows and snow-bedazzled peaks. And all participants can meet the darling canine athletes when they're not running. — *Heather Mundt*

Read more: bit.ly/roam2019colorado

Sierra Snow in Tahoe
Family fun beyond the slopes

I'm biased, but I can't think of a better winter family getaway than Lake Tahoe. With an average of 300 to 500 inches of fresh Sierra Nevada powder annually, most visitors head straight for the ski slopes. But what if you need a break from the mountain mayhem? Not a problem on the West Shore.

Want to snowshoe, snowmobile or snowbike? Do a ropes course in the snow? Ice skate or sleigh ride? Take a walk by the lake? Shop and eat in Truckee, the hippest California mountain town around? Or just stay near the cabin for snowball fights, snowman building and marshmallow toasting? — *Carolyn Jensen*

Read more: bit.ly/roam2019tahoe

Spring Breakin'

Atop the Bermuda Triangle
Outdoor adventure in the Atlantic

It's tough to believe that Bermuda used to be known only as a destination for the newly wed, almost-dead or over-fed. What used to be a playground for honeymooners, retirees, and cruise ship daytrippers is now one of the hottest islands in the world. After legalizing gay marriage and receiving accolades from the travel press, there is no doubt that the mid-Atlantic isle is drawing families and jetsetters at an eye-popping clip.

And it's easy to see why. After flying just two-and-a-half hours from the East Coast, our summer week in Bermuda was a blur of pink beaches, pirate grottos, bike trails, limestone caverns, and sparkling coves. We hiked, biked, swam and explored the picturesque and historic villages. The Bermudans were lovely ambassadors to their intoxicating mix of British, Caribbean, and American culture. Our teens could not get enough of the cliff jumps or the snorkeling. My husband and I loved the bright spirit and the rum swizzles. The only thing we missed in Bermuda? Any sign of "Triangle" mysteries. — *Jill Headley*

Read more: bit.ly/roam2019bermuda

Swimming in Maui
Paradise with purpose

It started with a fight. As my finger hovered over the online registration button for municipal swim lessons in San Francisco, my four-year-old daughter began to wail, "Noooo! I DO NOT want to take swim lessons here... I'll take swim lessons in Maui!"

Maybe she was right. What better place to get my daughter excited about swimming than in Maui, where we'd be surrounded by surf, sun, and water everywhere? Our trip wouldn't be a swim boot camp for preschoolers — it would be a vacation with a little added structure. I eagerly typed "swim lessons Maui" into Yelp. — *Maria De La O*

Read more: bit.ly/roam2019maui

Toddling through Guadalajara
Twins take on the heart of Mexico

I was so enchanted by Guadalajara. Five times bigger than my home of San Francisco, the city was percolating with energy, color, and wonderfully warm people. Guadalajara is the cultural center of Mexico and very well-equipped to welcome tourists, although I met very few. What a joy it was to see a true picture of Mexican city life.

The twins had a ball every day: listening to music, strolling plazas and churches, hanging out with a polar bear, and toddling until they crashed hard in their stroller. After our "Big City" days, we decamped for Lake Chapala and more fun and relaxation. It was a perfect family trip to the heart of Mexico. — *Darya Moore*

Read more: bit.ly/roam2019guadalajara

Take the Kids to Cuba
Not as "hot" but just as cool

As we prepped for our week in Cuba, a friend asked, "Wouldn't it be more fun without the kids? All those hot Havana nights? The clubs? The rum? The rhumba?"

The truth is, it never crossed our minds to leave our kids at home — and we didn't regret our decision for an instant. Right after the U.S. reopened Cuba to independent travel in 2015, Americans flocked to the island. And though the destination isn't as "hot" today, Cuba's people, cities, beaches, and mountains still deliver a once-in-a-lifetime family vacation — one we'll never forget.
— *Megan Harvey* and *Jodi Glasser*

Read more: bit.ly/roam2019cuba , bit.ly/roam2019oldcuba

Wet & Wild in Belize
Rough it — then relax it

If your dream family vacation involves a beach with the whitest sand and lightest water, get thee to Belize.

But Belize is so much more than just stunning beaches. We were looking for an eco-friendly escape in Central America, with some combination of roughing it and a few small luxuries. After a little more research, Belize won out — we wanted a more snorkel-friendly (rather than surf-friendly) beach experience for our 8-year-old and 6-year-old. Plus Belize's Mayan ruins and jungle adventures offered something new and unusual that we could all explore together.
— *Dina Harrison*

Read more: bit.ly/roam2019belize

THANKSGIVING FEASTS

Woodstock's Changing Colors
Autumn leaves fall in NY's Catskills

Woodstock and its adjacent towns have long been a draw for artists and nature-lovers of every stripe. Beginning with the Hudson River School painters and Arts & Crafts movement of the late 1800s, through the late '60s when Jimi Hendrix and Bob Dylan stayed here, to the present day, this corner of the Catskills has long beckoned edgy New Yorkers into the woods.
Here you'll find wealthy artists, a Buddhist monastery, yoga, a world-class film festival, and a "music chapel" in the woods, as well as a healthy dose of shops trading on the hippie past in Woodstock's town center. And with hangry kids in tow, the Hudson Valley is a foodie paradise with farm-to-table cuisine ruling the scene.

The best way to see the local flora and fauna is to get those kids out on the hiking trail, and since Woodstock is situated within Catskill Park where nearly half the land is protected by the state or by New York City, there are plenty of trails to choose from. Right in the middle of Woodstock, along Tannery Brook, is the little Woodstock Waterfall Park, a pocket park that overlooks a pretty spectacular waterfall, and about 20 minutes outside of the village is Mount Tremper, where you can find the Guinness book–certified largest kaleidoscope in the world. For a leaf-peep getaway, Woodstock won't disappoint. — *Maria De La O*

Read more: bit.ly/roam2019woodstock

Sushi for Thanksgiving?!
A perfect November in Tokyo & Kyoto

Our Chloe had begged to visit her longtime BFF since Mayuko had moved back to her native Tokyo after five years in the U.S. She was certain Japan and the Japanese would be as nice and wonderful as Mayuko's family. We were skeptical about a family vacation to one of the world's most crowded and expensive countries.

Save for our friendship with Mayuko's family, Japan would not have appeared on my family trip "bucket list." Though when Mayuko's parents extended an invitation, we jumped at the chance to reunite our daughters and booked a trip for Thanksgiving. Turns out, Chloe was absolutely right about Japan. — *Julie Rappaport*

Read more: bit.ly/roam2019japan

Get Yosemite to Yourself
Offseason has views without crowds

Most Californians I know will think nothing of fighting hours of bumper-to-bumper traffic to get to fresh powder in Tahoe or Mammoth — which is funny because just a tweak of the compass makes the traffic disappear and delivers a four-hour ride to heaven.

Yosemite National Park receives more than four million visitors each year but fewer than 10 percent of them come in the winter. Pick a non-holiday and you'll feel like you've got the place to yourself — especially compared to a summer visit. My 12-year-old daughter Pearl and I were lucky to spend a November weekend in Yosemite and Sequoia after the first snows of the season. And we'd do it again in a heartbeat. — *Maryann Jones Thompson*

Read more: bit.ly/roam2019yosemite

Fall Foliage in Pennsylvania
Autumn from the Kinzua Sky Walk

If you're planning a fall foliage road trip, avoid the major highways and head for the old country roads of Pennsylvania. Not only is the scenery better, but you'll get to see how peaceful it used to be to travel back in the day before the advent of the modern super-highway.

When it comes to fall foliage, you can't get much better than the Kinzua Sky Walk. Right around October, the lush, green hillsides begin to turn to various shades of bright yellow, red, and orange. Each year we pack the kids into the Hyundai and hit the old back country roads to experience Mother Nature's annual show of color and wonder erupt around the old railroad bridge — and each year we are blown away. — *Valentine J. Brkich*

Read more: bit.ly/roam2019pennsylvania

Cheap & Cozy Near San Francisco
Getaway for less in the Bay Area

By the time our kids were in elementary school, we realized Thanksgiving was the perfect time for a two-on-two, parent-kid break. So now we skip the hosting, unplug from devices, activities and friends, and head for the nearby hills. We take a hike, pass a football, play some cards, and basically, just chill out — just the four of us.

With the massive expenses of summer's travels not gone from memory and the massive expenses of Christmas looming, we aim for a cheap cabin that's no more than an hour from home — and preferably without wifi. Luckily, the San Francisco Bay Area has more than its share of cheap and cozy destinations awaiting your winter visit. — *Maryann Jones Thompson*

Read more: bit.ly/roam2019cheapcozy

DESTINATION 101

Barcelona — Again & Again & Again
Spain's superstar never disappoints

Have you ever cried when you walked inside a church? I hadn't either — until I stepped inside Sagrada Familia. I was surprised to be so emotional about a building — especially after visiting so many amazing cathedrals in Europe. Gaudi's stunner is an unfinished project that his followers have been working to complete for more than 100 years. And from its impossibly high ceilings to its rainbows of stained-glass to its tree-inspired pillars, Sagrada will move you.

And that's Barcelona, in a nutshell: Everything is over-the-top amazing. After many summers exploring Europe pre- and post-kids, Barcelona is my very favorite city. I visit again and again and never get enough. And after two trips and nearly two weeks there over two years, I bet my kids would want to go back again.

Why? My daughter and I are now avowed Gaudi freaks. We loved Casa Batl, Guell Palace and Casa Mila — but there's more to see! We loved strolling neighborhoods — El Raval, Barri Gotic, and Gracia. The beach is close enough for an afternoon dip. And you can imagine the food and drink — wow. Don't even get me started... The meat cones from the Boqueria market? We ate ten in nothing flat. I was so happy I wanted to cry. — *Dina Harrison*

Read more: bit.ly/roam2019barcelona

Waikiki with Everyone
Multigenerational perfection in Oahu

When my stepdad suggested we surprise my mom with a family trip to Oahu, I was tempted. When he offered up a week in one of my parents' timeshares, I was sold. After a lifetime in California, we were finally heading to Hawaii with the kids! The excitement was palpable.

My brother's family came along too — and their timeshare had a better view. I wasn't bitter (except I was) because the units were right in downtown Waikiki across the street from the beach. Over our week together, we found Oahu has got everything everyone needs for a perfect multigenerational trip — from gardens to shopping to beaches to restaurants to history. It was a trip we'll never forget. — *Amy Jones*

Read more: bit.ly/roam2019oahu

Buenos Aires with Kids
World-class heroes, cuisine, art & sports

It is nearly impossible to visit Buenos Aires without being inundated with images of the former first lady and beloved national symbol, Eva (Evita) Perón. After days in this amazing city, my 7-year-old daughter was officially hooked: Elsa is out, Evita is in.

While Evita is now firmly embedded in our family's psyche, so too is Argentina's capital. Buenos Aires is difficult to characterize and impossible to forget. I knew my husband and I would love it, but I was thrilled to see my kids equally charmed. With famous footballers, prolific street art, gorgeous parks, Malbecs, and dulce de leche, there is a lot to love for every member of the family. — *Sarah Hart*

Read more: bit.ly/roam2019buenosaires

Yachting the Caribbean
Not just for the rich & famous

Chartering a private yacht allows you to hire a captain to sail your family and friends through the tropical islands of your choice — all chef-prepared meals and drinks included. Spend your days snorkeling sky blue water and combing deserted beaches, and your nights in secluded coves stargazing or at beachfront reggae parties. No wonder the pirates loved the Caribbean.

The best part? You'll get all this for not much more than it would cost to take a family group on a nice cruise with 4,000 other people. After 15 years running a free yacht brokerage service, Nancy Van Winter of ENVY Yacht Charters shares her insight on what families can do to ensure a great charter experience.
— *Maryann Jones Thompson*

Read more: bit.ly/roam2019yacht

Best Beaches in Bali
Still-special spots by the sea

Bali is a remarkable place to spend a family holiday. The Balinese cultural spirit remains surprisingly legitimate despite decades of increasing tourism. This is especially obvious in Ubud, which remains a must-stop for temples and monkeys and dance performances and yoga set among the rice paddies.

When it's time to head for the beach, however, parents should push past the "crazy" to find smaller, simpler spots to spend your nights by the sea. After much research and a bit of trial-and-error, we found five family-friendly beach spots around the island. What we gave up in tour buses, nightclubs and offers to have our hair braided, we made up for in empty beaches, world-class snorkeling, and epic sunsets.
— *Maryann Jones Thompson*

Read more: bit.ly/roam2019bali

The Good Life in Vancouver

Squeezing all the charm into three days

It's tough to squeeze all the charm of BC's capital into a weekend–but it's worth a try. After our weekend, we learned Vancouver is a spectacularly beautiful city with a cost of living to match. With hip neighborhoods, epic outdoor adventures and delicious, eclectic food, why wouldn't you want to live there?

Start your adventure by gathering your courage and taking an unsteady walk across the 230 foot high Capilano Suspension Bridge. Afterwards, head to the 1,000-plus acre Stanley Park. Bordering downtown and home to the Vancouver Aquarium, this gorgeous park really does have something for everyone.

Get an overview of the park by grabbing bikes or running shoes and heading to the Seawall path. With 14 miles of stunning scenery, it's a great way to see the park, Granville Island, Kitsilano Beach, and the Burrard Inlet.

After your ride, take an aquabus to beautiful Granville Island. Once just warehouses and factories, this neighborhood has seen some serious urban revitalization and is now home to a public market and a kids market as well as galleries, shops and restaurants.
— *Sarah Hart*

Read more:
bit.ly/roam2019vancouver

QUICK PICKS

Layover in Dubai

Marvel at golden dunes and golden cars

Why stop in London if you can stop in Dubai? When choosing a flight for our summer vacation in South Africa, we decided to fly Emirates and make the most of its hub, one of the United Arab Emirates perched on the Persian Gulf. In just 36 hours, our family was able to ride camels on the must-do desert safari, "dune bash" in a truck "sandboard" on a snowboard, ascend the world's tallest building, Burj Kalifa, and explore Jumeirah Beach–none of which you can do when you layover near Heathrow.

Even though my boys' favorite Dubai memory was probably seeing a gold Lamborghini, I think the best part of our layover was being immersed in the culture.
— *Emily Janowsky*

Read more: bit.ly/roam2019dubai

Partying with Cranes in Lodi
Big birds and big wines draw thousands

All the sandhill cranes are doing it. Yep, the "greaters," the "lessers" — even the "Canadians" come to Lodi every winter for a massive sandhill crane party. As busy Californians zoom by on highways just south of Sacramento, birders from around the world are bundled up against the chilly delta breeze in an almost-dark field watching thousands of the four- and five-foot-tall birds fly in to party for the winter.

When we visited in early November, approximately 7,000 cranes were in town. By February, more than 25,000 arrive in the area nightly — the party gets hotter as winter gets colder.
— *Maryann Jones Thompson*

Read more: *bit.ly/roam2019lodi*

Boardwalk Empire
on the Jersey Shore
Asbury Park's got beaches and bohemia

Being a West Coaster, I'm always surprised that the East Coast holds so tightly to its traditions. As a Californian I love going to places off-season to avoid the crowds, but it's gotten me into trouble on the East Coast, where one risks having no place for a pit stop, much less a place to eat a bowl of clams.

Not so for Asbury Park, a revitalizing bohemian enclave on the Jersey Shore that extends its beach season just a little longer than most. Kids will love the tiny waves and tiny clams. Adults will love the food and vintage seaside spirit. — *Maria De La O*

Read more: *bit.ly/roam2019jerseyshore*

Country Bliss in Nashville
Finding new boots
& new friends in Tennessee

While boarding our flight home to Los Angeles, I overheard a woman saying, "Well, Nashville wasn't that great..."

I was shocked. My neck jerked around to lay eyes on the person who had uttered those words. I wanted to hug that poor darling, grab her by the hand, sit her down and ask her where in the world she had been? Her words did not make sense.

My daughter and I were at the end of a fabulous week in Nashville, filled with country music, Tennessee nature, ridiculously good food, cowboy boot shopping and — best of all, Southern hospitality.

The town of Nashville is so different from our home in LA — the culture is different, the landscape is different, the people are different and the language is different. In California, we are always in a hurry. In Tennessee, people move slower. They're less into their technology and more into their manners; they mow their lawns, sweep their stoops and relax on their porches.

I honestly can't imagine who that woman on the plane was hanging out with or where she went. Our time in Tennessee was heavenly. — *Renee Siegel*

Read more: *bit.ly/roam2019nashville*

10 PERFECT PARENT ESCAPES

ABSENCE MAKES THE HEART GROW FONDER – RIGHT?

From babies who can't sleep to teens who can't wake up, kids can be challenging. So when parents need a vacation from being parents, there's no itinerary needed. Just pick a great destination and the rest of the trip falls into place. After a stay at one of these ROAM picks, and you'll come home a better parent. We promise.

Read More: bit.ly/roam2019parentescapes

Havaiki Pearl, Fakarava, French Polynesia

Just an hour's flight from Tahiti, a beachfront bungalow awaits, with friendly service, French meals, crazy diving, and friendly sharks. It is relaxing — I swear!

Hotel Caruso, Ravello, Italy

Pretend you are Italian royalty in this romantic former palace set atop a cliff overlooking the Amalfi Coast.

W Austin, Texas

Hang your hat and hit the streets for Texas' best live music, BBQ, gospel and bars.

Nick's Cove, Marshall, California

Across from Point Reyes in the rolling green hills of West Marin, Nick's Cove cottages sit on Tomales Bay, serving local seafood and serious serenity.

Red Mountain Resort, St. George, Utah

Go alone. Go with your partner. Go with your friends. This destination in the red rocks near Zion National Park provides yogic, meditative, massaged peace and/or heart-pumping activities, depending on your preference.

Conrad Maldives, Rangali Island

Forget the overwater bungalows, the Rangali now has an underwater bungalow! But the plain old beach bungalows are beyond amazing for a super special couples trip.

Hotel Monteleone, New Orleans

You can't go wrong in New Orleans, and you can't go wrong at the classic Hotel Monteleone. Trip around the Garden District, love some jazz, eat yourself silly and wrap up the night at the famous Carousel Bar.

The Surfrider, Malibu, California

Pretend you're a local and settle in for some sets at First Point and some sunsets from the boho-style roof deck at this rejuvenated PCH mainstay.

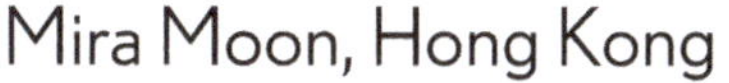

Mira Moon, Hong Kong

Bask in the energy only Hong Kong can deliver during a stay at the Mira Moon, Wanchai's home for mixing old- and new-world traditions from both the East and the West.

Le Domaine de L'Orangeraie, La Digue, Seychelles

Okay, you can certainly bring your kids here. But wouldn't it be cool to just while away your days, lazing beside the Indian Ocean? Maybe break it up with a bike ride or a glass of champagne? Yes, yes it would.

"After 13-hours in a Jeep with our tiny daughters, Jose and I reached the remote Zanskar Valley, a high-altitude region in the Himalayas of Northern India. We came for the hikes, monasteries, and scenery, but we found the real reward was experiencing the culture of the region's ethnically Tibetan villages-communities left untouched by Chinese influence.

We were lucky to be in the area for an annual festival at a remote monastery that brought out everyone in their best traditional dress.

There were two professional photographers at the celebration, but their tons of gear looked alien and almost intrusive among the local festival. The villagers pushed them into a corner even as they welcomed our family with open arms.

It was amazing to interact with so many locals-and we were even invited for dinner with a local family afterward. None of these experiences would have been possible if we weren't traveling as a family."

LILIIA DECOS

ROAM 2019 Best Family Travel Photo Contest Winner

"I'm a big believer in winging it. I'm a big believer that you're never going to find a perfect city travel experience or the perfect meal without a constant willingness to experience a bad one. Letting the happy accident happen is what a lot of vacation itineraries miss, I think, and I'm always trying to push people to allow those things to happen rather than stick to some rigid itinerary."

— ANTHONY BOURDAIN

REAL FAMILIES
REAL ADVENTURES
REAL FUN

Ever wonder how ordinary families take *extraordinary* vacations?

We did. So ROAM spent years gathering tales from intrepid parent travelers who've taken their kids to off-the-theme-park-track spots and publishing the details on **ROAMFamilyTravel.com.**

And though we wanted to know the "where," we were equally intrigued by the "how." How do families find resources to plan, take and pay for incredible journeys in today's crazy-busy world?

Whether campers in the mountains or sailors in the tropics, ROAMing families have three things in common: They make travel a priority, they believe time together is the best part, and they devote a ton of time to independent planning and research.

ROAM's Journal of Real Family Adventure aims to make unique vacations easier to take. In the following pages, veteran travelers share the highs, lows, and must-knows from more than fifty exciting trips around the world, with links to more information online.

What you won't find is any professional photos or marketing copy: All the images, stories, and tips are from the parents who've been there, so you'll know you can follow in their footsteps.

Let's ROAM!

MARYANN JONES THOMPSON

ROAM Founder & Editor in Chief
San Francisco, California, June 2019